Mental Health Screening and Monitoring for Children in Care

Mental Health Screening and Monitoring for Children in Care provides a concise, step-by-step guide for children's agencies on how to carry out mental health screening and monitoring for children and adolescents growing up in alternative care.

Michael Tarren-Sweeney outlines unique universal mental health screening and monitoring procedures that can be implemented without the need for clinical training or professional oversight. These procedures reliably identify which children should be referred to clinical services for a comprehensive assessment, and which children do not require further assessment. Informed by recent empirical research carried out with children in foster care in Australia and the Netherlands, these procedures screen the vast majority of children who have clinical-level difficulties for a second-stage assessment, including those with attachment- and trauma-related difficulties, meaning that very few such children remain undetected.

This book is an invaluable resource for charitable children's agencies, children's service providers, statutory children's services, children's social workers, and post-adoption support services.

Michael Tarren-Sweeney is a clinical child psychologist, epidemiologist, and child developmental theorist. He is Professor of Child and Family Psychology at Canterbury University in New Zealand, and founding Editor of the international research journal *Developmental Child Welfare*.

Mental Health Screening and Monitoring for Children in Care

A Short Guide for Children's Agencies and Post-adoption Services

Michael Tarren-Sweeney

Routledge
Taylor & Francis Group

LONDON AND NEW YORK

First published 2019
by Routledge
2 Park Square, Milton Park, Abingdon, Oxon OX14 4RN

and by Routledge
711 Third Avenue, New York, NY 10017

Routledge is an imprint of the Taylor & Francis Group, an informa
business

© 2019 Michael Tarren-Sweeney

The right of Michael Tarren-Sweeney to be identified as author of this
work has been asserted by him in accordance with sections 77 and 78
of the Copyright, Designs and Patents Act 1988.

All rights reserved. No part of this book may be reprinted or
reproduced or utilised in any form or by any electronic, mechanical,
or other means, now known or hereafter invented, including
photocopying and recording, or in any information storage or retrieval
system, without permission in writing from the publishers.

Trademark notice: Product or corporate names may be trademarks
or registered trademarks, and are used only for identification and
explanation without intent to infringe.

British Library Cataloguing-in-Publication Data
A catalogue record for this book is available from the British Library

Library of Congress Cataloging-in-Publication Data
Names: Tarren-Sweeney, Michael, author.
Title: Mental health screening and monitoring for children in care :
   a short guide for children's agencies and post-adoption services /
   Michael Tarren-Sweeney.
Description: Milton Park, Abingdon, Oxon ; New York, NY :
   Routledge, 2018. | Includes bibliographical references and index.
Identifiers: LCCN 2018009996 | ISBN 9781138104716 (hbk :
   alk. paper) | ISBN 9781138104730 (pbk : alk. paper) |
   ISBN 9781315102078 (ebk : alk. paper)
Subjects: LCSH: Child mental health services—Handbooks, manuals, etc. |
   Foster children—Mental health. | Mental status examination.
Classification: LCC RJ499.3 .T37 2018 | DDC 362.2083—dc23
LC record available at https://lccn.loc.gov/2018009996

ISBN: 978-1-138-10471-6 (hbk)
ISBN: 978-1-138-10473-0 (pbk)
ISBN: 978-1-315-10207-8 (ebk)

Typeset in Bembo
by Apex CoVantage, LLC
Printed and bound by CPI Group (UK) Ltd, Croydon CR0 4YY

For my darling Georgie,
And our three wonderful children,
With all my love

Contents

List of figures

List of tables

Acknowledgements

I wish to acknowledge my dear colleague Anouk Goemans (of Leiden University, The Netherlands), who has kept me focussed on the technicalities of mental health screening for children in care, and who collaborated on the screening protocol in Chapter 5.

This book includes extracts of text, as well as some tables and figures that were first published in the following articles and chapters:

Tarren-Sweeney, M., Goemans, A., van Geel, M., Vedder, P., Hahne, A.S., & Gieve, M. (in press). Mental health screening for children in care using the Strengths and Difficulties Questionnaire and the Brief Assessment Checklists: Guidance from three national studies. *Developmental Child Welfare*.

Tarren-Sweeney, M. (2017). Mental health services for our most vulnerable children. *Clinical Child Psychology & Psychiatry*, *22*(4), 521–523.

Tarren-Sweeney, M. (2017). Rates of meaningful change in the mental health of children in long-term out-of-home care: A seven- to nine-year prospective study. *Child Abuse & Neglect*, *72*, 1–9.

Tarren-Sweeney, M. (2016). The developmental case for adopting children from care. *Clinical Child Psychology and Psychiatry*, *21*(4), 497–505.

Tarren-Sweeney, M. (2014). Our twenty first century quest: Locating effective mental health interventions for children and young people in care, and those adopted from care. In M. Tarren-Sweeney & A. Vetere (Eds.), *Mental health services for vulnerable children and young people: Supporting children who are, or have been, in foster care*. London: Routledge.

Tarren-Sweeney, M., & Vetere, A. (2014). Establishing the need for mental health services for children and young people in care, and those who are subsequently adopted. In M. Tarren-Sweeney & A. Vetere (Eds.), *Mental health services for vulnerable children and young people: Supporting children who are, or have been, in foster care*. London: Routledge.

Tarren-Sweeney, M. (2013). The Assessment Checklist for Adolescents (ACA): A scale for measuring the mental health of young people in foster, kinship, residential and adoptive care. *Children and Youth Services Review, 35*, 384–393.

Tarren-Sweeney, M. (2013). The Brief Assessment Checklists (BAC-C, BAC-A): Mental health screening measures for school-aged children and adolescents in foster, kinship, residential and adoptive care. *Children and Youth Services Review, 35*(5), 771–779.

Tarren-Sweeney, M. (2013). An investigation of complex attachment- and trauma-related symptomatology among children in foster and kinship care. *Child Psychiatry and Human Development, 44*, 727–741.

Tarren-Sweeney, M. (2010). An exploratory investigation of abnormal pain response among pre-adolescent children in foster care. *Clinical Child Psychology and Psychiatry, 15*(1), 65–79.

Tarren-Sweeney, M. (2010). Concordance of mental health impairment and service utilisation among children in care. *Clinical Child Psychology and Psychiatry, 15*(4), 481–495.

Tarren-Sweeney, M. (2010). It's time to re-think mental health services for children in care, and those adopted from care. *Clinical Child Psychology and Psychiatry, 15*(4), 613–626.

Tarren-Sweeney, M. (2008). Predictors of problematic sexual behaviour among children with complex maltreatment histories. *Child Maltreatment, 13*, 182–198.

Tarren-Sweeney, M. (2008). Retrospective and concurrent predictors of the mental health of children in care. *Children and Youth Services Review, 30*, 1–25.

Tarren-Sweeney, M. (2007). The Assessment Checklist for Children–ACC: A behavioural rating scale for children in foster, residential and kinship care. *Children and Youth Services Review, 29*, 672–691.

Tarren-Sweeney, M. (2006). Patterns of aberrant eating among pre-adolescent children in foster care. *Journal of Abnormal Child Psychology, 34*, 623–634.

Tarren-Sweeney, M., Hazell, P., & Carr, V. (2004). Are foster parents reliable informants of children's behaviour problems? *Child: Care, Health and Development, 30*(2), 167–175.

Abbreviations

ACA	Assessment Checklist for Adolescents
ACA-SF	Assessment Checklist for Adolescents – Short Form
ACC	Assessment Checklist for Children
ACC-SF	Assessment Checklist for Children – Short Form
ACC+	Assessment Checklist for Children – Plus
ACP-SF	Assessment Checklist for Preschoolers – Short Form
ADHD	Attention-deficit hyperactivity disorder
APR	Abnormal pain response
ASEBA	Achenbach System of Empirically Based Assessment
ASQ:SE	Ages and Stages Questionnaire, Social and Emotional
AUC	Area under the curve
BAC-A	Brief Assessment Checklist for Adolescents
BAC-C	Brief Assessment Checklist for Children
BASC3-BESS	BASC-3 Behavioral and Emotional Screening System
BITSEA	Brief Infant-Toddler Social and Emotional Assessment
BPM	Brief Problem Monitor
CAMHS	Child and Adolescent Mental Health Services
CBCL	Child Behavior Checklist
CICS	Children in Care Study
CIS	Client Information System

CSA	Child sexual abuse
DSM	*Diagnostic and Statistical Manual for Mental Disorders* (various editions)
HSS	Hyperphagic short stature
ICD	*International Classification of Diseases*
LAAC	Looked after and adopted children
MTFC	Multidimensional treatment foster care
NHS	National Health Service
NSCAW	National Survey of Child and Adolescent Well-Being
NSW	New South Wales (Australian state)
OOHC	Out-of-home care
PTSD	Post traumatic stress disorder
RAD	Reactive attachment disorder
ROC	Receiver operating characteristics
SBP	Sexual behaviour problems
SDQ	Strengths and Difficulties Questionnaire
TRF	Teacher Report Form
YSR	Youth Self Report

Preface

I wrote this book with one purpose in mind: to improve the detection of mental ill health among children growing up in various forms of alternative care. This includes common types of mental health problems that public child and adolescent mental health services are most familiar with, but also less common attachment- and trauma-related problems that are mainly observed among children with histories of maltreatment, including those placed into alternative care. Children's agencies have a moral and legal duty of care to monitor and ensure the psychological well-being of children residing in alternative care. Yet many governments allocate the responsibilities for *social care* and for *clinical assessment and therapeutic services* (for this population) to different agencies. Several Australian state child welfare departments maintain their own psychological services such that they can deliver both social work and psychological services to children that are in their statutory care. But in most western jurisdictions, public provision of clinical assessment and therapeutic services for children in statutory care is the responsibility of health ministries. A dilemma arises from the fact that public child and adolescent mental health services tend to match their intake criteria to their funded service capacity. Over time, the threshold at which children and/or their caregivers are accepted for therapeutic services has diverged from the threshold at which such families need or would manifestly benefit from such services.

The remedy that I propose in this book, while imperfect, aims for the transparent identification of such need. The systematic identification of children in alternative care requiring comprehensive mental health assessment by clinical services has social policy and political implications, extending beyond the needs of individual children. Ignoring or 'burying' a problem is a timeless political strategy, while spotlighting the problem removes political cover. Public health services are presently more overloaded than ever, a consequence of decades of underfunding, and of medical and technological advances that carry hefty price tags. In the present climate, the substantial treatment needs of children growing up in alternative care will only be acknowledged and attended to if they are glaringly visible to health services and policy makers.

And so, this book encourages children's agencies to proactively identify which of the children in their charge show sufficient signs of poor mental health to signal the need for a comprehensive clinical/development assessment. There are two reasons why we should do this. First, we have a duty of care to identify those children whose development and well-being is compromised by poor mental health, regardless of whether there are enough clinical services to attend to these children or not. And second, we have a duty to highlight shortfalls in essential mental health services for society's most vulnerable children.

Michael Tarren-Sweeney

1 The mental health of children and young people in alternative care

Who are children and young people in alternative care?

Children residing in statutory care are collectively referred to as *looked after* children in Britain and Ireland, and as children in *out-of-home care* in North America and Australasia. Neither term satisfactorily describes the status of children in long-term statutory care. Increasing numbers of such children exit statutory care to legally permanent placements with caregivers who are not their birth parents under various types of guardianship and adoption orders. These child populations are differentiated by their legal status but not their developmental histories. They have similar need for social and clinical support services. Yet because of their differing legal status, governments have not tended to view them collectively. This book purposely treats them as a single population defined by shared developmental and social histories, namely children and young people in *alternative care* – a collective term promoted by the United Nations (United Nations General Assembly, 2010). The United Nations employs the term *alternative care* to encompass all forms of non-parental care provided to children, including that which is legally sanctioned or not (informal care arrangements); that which is meant to be long-term or temporary; and that which is legally permanent or legally impermanent, *except adoption*. However, in this book the collective term 'alternative care' encompasses *adoption from statutory care*.

Maltreated children who have an ongoing need for care

The protection, psychological development, and well-being of a large majority of maltreated children is best served through varying levels and types of family support services, including specialized parenting interventions and parental drug and alcohol treatment. It goes without saying that providing effective family supports earlier, rather than later, is the key to arresting and preventing further developmental harm for such children. A relatively small proportion of children who are maltreated (abused and/or neglected) by their parents or other guardians have an *ongoing need for alternative care*. These are children who tend to experience more severe, more chronic, more pervasive, and more diverse maltreatment. The care their parents provide falls well short of 'good enough'. What differentiates them from other seriously maltreated children is that their parents' caregiving is not sufficiently amenable to change (e.g. by way of parenting interventions) within developmentally critical timeframes. Figure 1.1

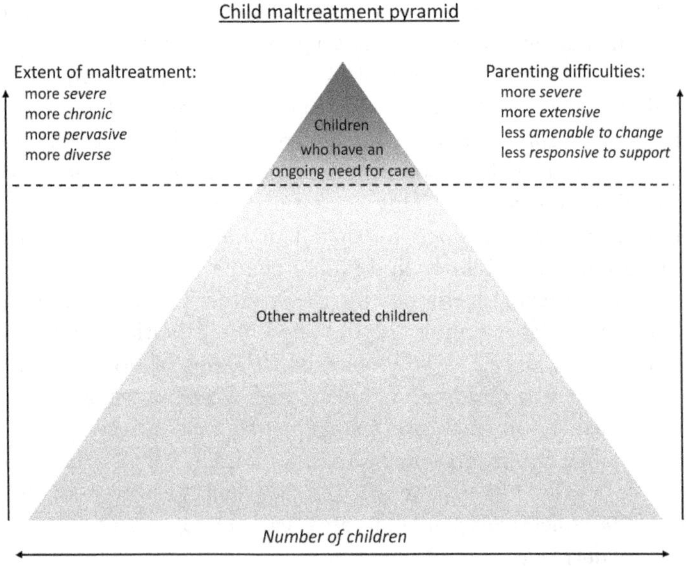

Figure 1.1 Child maltreatment pyramid

provides a diagrammatic representation of these children in relation to other maltreated children.

Within a family preservation framework, the primary purpose of statutory (out-of-home) care is to provide maltreated children temporary protective care, with restoration to their parents being the ultimate goal. Since the 1970s it has been apparent that an increasing proportion of children placed into care either cannot, or should not, be returned home. The observation that many of these children subsequently 'drift' in care without acquiring relational permanence, highlighted a concern for the developmental well-being of children growing up in *impermanent* out-of-home care (Fein & Maluccio, 1992; Rowe & Lambert, 1973). While this has prompted a policy shift in favour of legally permanent placements for children who cannot be safely returned to their parents, large proportions of children placed into legally impermanent out-of-home care remain thus until adulthood (Biehal, Ellison, Baker, & Sinclair, 2010). This reality raises important questions about the developmental well-being of children who grow up in impermanent statutory care, and the extent to which our present models of care support or hinder children's recovery from early developmental adversity.

At any given time, perhaps a million children in the western world either reside in statutory out-of-home care or have exited such care to adoption or other permanent orders. A substantially larger population encounters these types of alternative care at some time in their childhood.

What proportions of children in alternative care have clinically meaningful mental health difficulties?

Surveys have consistently found that a child in care is more likely than not to have psychological difficulties of sufficient scale or severity to require mental health services, regardless of which country they reside in (Tarren-Sweeney, 2008a). Children in care also endure poorer physical health, higher prevalence of learning and language difficulties, and poorer educational outcomes than other children (Crawford, 2006). More than 30 surveys in North America, Europe, and Australia have reported that children and young people placed in statutory (i.e. out-of-home) alternative care experience much higher levels and rates of mental health difficulties than do children at large (Oswald, Heil, & Goldbeck, 2010; Pecora, White, Jackson, & Wiggins, 2009). These survey estimates are mainly derived from standard caregiver-report rating scales – primarily the Child Behavior Checklist (CBCL; Achenbach & Rescorla, 2001), the Strengths and Difficulties Questionnaire (SDQ; Goodman, 2001), and the Rutter Scales (Elander & Rutter, 1996). This is largely accounted for by pre-care exposure to maltreatment, emotional deprivation, and disrupted attachments (Rutter, 2000). Indeed, the scale and complexity of their mental health difficulties is unparalleled among populations defined by family history and legal status rather than psychological development. Although rates vary a little by survey and location, between 35% and 50% of children in care have clinical-level mental health difficulties, and another 15% to 25% have difficulties approaching clinical significance. The scale of their mental health difficulties more closely resembles that of clinic-referred children than of children at large.

Rates for different types of alternative care

Although there is considerable variation in care systems, most western jurisdictions shifted emphasis from non-family residential care to foster care through the late 20th century, and more recently to kinship care. The latter trend is partly driven in Australia, New Zealand, and Canada by concern for the identity and well-being of large and disproportionate numbers of indigenous children in care.

Residential care

The small proportion of children placed in residential care have much higher average levels of mental health difficulties and higher rates of mental disorders (Hukkanen, Sourander, Bergroth, & Piha, 1999; Meltzer, Corbin, Gatward, Goodman, & Ford, 2003). This is because residential care is largely reserved for children whose behavioural and social relationship difficulties make family-based care less sustainable – typically following a sequence of placement disruptions. This differentiation is less evident in countries that have retained large residential care systems, such as France (where half of children in care are placed in residential group homes). A recent French survey of adolescents in residential care ($N = 183$) found that 49% had one or more mental disorders − 2.5 to 3.5 times the rate among French children at large (Bronsard et al., 2011). This is lower than that reported in systems where much smaller proportions of young people are placed in residential care, and is more consistent with estimated rates of disorder for children and youth in foster care.

Kinship care

Conversely, among children residing in family-based statutory care, those placed with kin have lower rates of clinical-level difficulties than those placed with unrelated foster families (Delfabbro, 2016; Holtan, Ronning, Handegård, & Sourander, 2005; Vanschoonlandt, Vanderfaeillie, Van Holen, De Maeyer, & Andries, 2012). The reasons for this are unclear. All other things being equal, children clearly stand to benefit from being raised within their extended biological families. However, these findings are also likely to be partly accounted for by selection effects − whereby children with fewer difficulties are more likely to be sustained in kinship placements. Among the participants of my longitudinal Children in Care Study, many more had transferred from kinship placements to foster placements than in the opposite direction.

Adoption from care

Two recent studies in the United Kingdom measured surprisingly high levels of mental health difficulties among population samples of children adopted from care − comparable to that experienced by children who remain in foster care (De Jong, Hodges, & Malik, 2016; Selwyn, Wijedasa, & Meakings, 2014). These findings confirm the need for post-adoption support services and dispel the notion that children in statutory care who are selected for adoption have fewer psychological and developmental difficulties than those remaining in long-term foster care.

What types and patterns of mental health difficulties are observed among children in alternative care?

More is known about the scale and prevalence of mental health difficulties experienced by children and young people in various forms of alternative care than of the nature, patterns, and complexity of those difficulties. This is largely because most available research data were obtained as outcome measures in studies addressing non-clinical research questions. More than 30 such studies have measured children's mental health outcomes using standard parent-report survey rating scales, notably the CBCL and the SDQ. These surveys have established that children in alternative care have very high rates of externalizing, internalizing, and attentional difficulties, and proportionately low prosocial behaviour. Diagnostic surveys have also estimated a high prevalence of conduct disorder (17%–45%), attention-deficit hyperactivity disorder (10%–30%), depression (4%–36%), post traumatic stress disorder (40%–50%), and generalized anxiety disorder (4%–26%) among mixed samples of children and young people in foster and residential care (Blower, Addo, Hodgson, Lamington, & Towlson, 2004Dubner & Motta, 1999; Famularo & Augustyn, 1996; McCann, Wilson, & Dunn, 1996; McMillen et al., 2005; Stein, Rae-Grant, Ackland, & Avison, 1994). A recent population survey estimated the following rates of *Diagnostic and Statistical Manual* (4th edition; DSM-IV) mental disorders among a sample of 279 6- to 12-year-old Norwegian children: any disorder = 50.9%; emotional disorders = 24.0%; attention-deficit/hyperactivity disorder = 19.0%; behavioural disorders = 21.5%; and reactive attachment disorder = 19.4% (Lehmann, Havik, Havik, & Heiervang, 2013).

In recent decades, the mental health of children in alternative care has tended to be framed in terms of the problems measured in population surveys by the CBCL and SDQ, specifically aggression, inattention, and emotional problems – while relationship and trauma-related difficulties have been overlooked. These under-researched problems include attachment-related difficulties, anxiety and dissociative responses to trauma, age-inappropriate sexual behaviour, and self-harm. Yet this was not always so. Early accounts of children in institutional care emphasized their disturbed relationship styles, accompanied by aggressive behaviour, low empathy, and hyperactivity (Wolkind & Rushton, 1994). This was variously described as "affectionless psychopathy" (Bender & Yarnell, 1941), "the affect hungry child" (Levy, 1937), and "institutional syndrome" (Goldfarb, 1949). More recently, research on the problems of Romanian adoptees has revived an interest in the nature of attachment difficulties and inattention/hyperactivity among infants raised in residential care (Kreppner et al., 2001; O'Connor, Bredenkamp, Rutter, & the English and Romanian Adoptees Study Team, 1999).

The Assessment Checklist measures were developed by the author to measure these under-researched mental health difficulties. The remainder of this chapter describes the types and patterns of mental health difficulties experienced by children in foster and kinship care, as measured by the Assessment Checklist measures and the CBCL, in a longitudinal, epidemiological study: the Children in Care Study (CICS).

The Assessment Checklist measures

The Assessment Checklist for Children (ACC)

The Assessment Checklist for Children (ACC) is a 120-item caregiver-report rating scale measuring maladaptive behaviours, emotional states, traits, and manners of relating to others that are experienced among children in alternative care. The ACC's content was developed systematically, with a view to measuring all clinically significant problems experienced by children in alternative care that are not adequately measured by standard parent-report checklists such as the CBCL and SDQ. Initial data indicate that the instrument has good content, construct, and criterion-related validity (Tarren-Sweeney, 2007). The ACC has 10 clinical scales and two low self-esteem scales that were empirically derived through factor analysis.

The ACC clinical scales are:

   I Sexual behaviour
  II Pseudomature interpersonal behaviour
 III Non-reciprocal interpersonal behaviour
 IV Indiscriminate interpersonal behaviour

  V   Insecure interpersonal behaviour
 VI   Anxious – distrustful
VII   Abnormal pain response
VIII Food maintenance behaviour
 IX   Self-injury
  X   Suicide discourse.

The ACC low self-esteem scales are:

 I   Negative self-image
 II   Low confidence.

The ACC Clinical Scale I measures age-inappropriate sexual behaviour. Scales II to V measure various forms of maladaptive interpersonal relatedness which are suggestive of attachment disorder behaviours and/or attachment-related social difficulties. Scale II describes a pattern of precious pseudomaturity and role reversal. Scale III describes emotionally withdrawn, avoidant, and non-reciprocal social behaviours, with high scores being suggestive of a severely avoidant-insecure attachment style and/or inhibited form of reactive attachment disorder. Scale IV describes a pattern of indiscriminate overfriendliness, and affection-seeking and attention-seeking behaviours, resembling the disinhibited form of reactive attachment disorder. Scale V measures a range of social behaviours and emotional difficulties suggestive of felt insecurity that is likely to reflect both trait insecurity (insecure attachment, temperament) and state insecurity (e.g. as a response to severe stressors, such as impermanent care). Scale VI measures a pattern of trauma-related anxiety and distrust. Scale VII measures a pattern of abnormal responses to physical hurt suggestive of pain insensitivity or failure to communicate felt pain. Scale VIII measures a pattern of excessive eating and food acquisition (termed *food maintenance syndrome*), which appears to be primarily triggered by acute stress and which resembles the behavioural correlates of hyperphagic short stature. Scale IX primarily measures various types of self-injurious behaviour but also measures three pica-type behaviours. Scale X measures suicidal talk, attempted suicide, and some other behaviours indicating risk for self-harm. The ACC Low Self-Esteem Scale I measures self-evaluations that suggest the child has a profoundly negative self-image, while Scale II measures self-evaluations that suggest a child is easily discouraged and lacks confidence in their social, educational, or other abilities.

The Assessment Checklist for Adolescents (ACA)

The Assessment Checklist for Adolescents (ACA) is a 105-item caregiver-report variant of the ACC, designed to measure maladaptive behaviours, emotional states, traits, and manners of relating to others that are experienced among 12- to 17-year-old young people in various forms of alternative care. The ACA was designed to measure a broad range of mental health difficulties observed among young people in alternative care that are not adequately measured by standard rating instruments, such as the CBCL, SDQ, and Conners Scales. Initial data indicate that the ACA has good content, construct, and criterion-related validity as well as high internal reliability (Tarren-Sweeney, 2013). While the ACA's content is mostly derived from the ACC, its factor structure differs from that of the ACC. The ACA has seven clinical scales and two low self-esteem scales that were empirically derived through factor analysis:

The ACA clinical scales are:

    I Non-reciprocal interpersonal behaviour
   II Social instability/behavioural dysregulation
  III Emotional dysregulation/distorted social cognition
  IV Dissociation/trauma symptoms
   V Food maintenance behaviour
  VI Sexual behaviour
 VII Suicide discourse.

The ACA low self-esteem scales are:

I   Negative self-image
II   Low confidence.

The ACA Clinical Scale I describes emotionally withdrawn, avoidant, and non-reciprocal social behaviours, with high scores being suggestive of a severely avoidant-insecure attachment style and/or inhibited form of reactive attachment disorder. Scale II describes a complex combination of unstable, attachment-related social relatedness difficulties and behavioural dysregulation. This scale incorporates the majority of items contained in the ACC Pseudomature and Indiscriminate scales. Scale III describes a pattern of highly dysregulated emotion and affective instability, coupled with distorted social cognition (negative attributions, paranoid beliefs). Scale IV measures a pattern of trauma-related dissociation and anxiety symptoms. Scale V measures a pattern of excessive eating and food acquisition (termed *food maintenance syndrome*), which appears to be primarily triggered by acute stress, and which resembles the behavioural correlates of hyperphagic short stature. Scale VI measures age-inappropriate sexual behaviour. Scale VII measures suicidal talk, attempted suicide, and some other behaviours indicating risk for self-harm. The ACA Low Self-Esteem Scale I measures self-evaluations that suggest the child has a profoundly negative self-image, while Scale II measures self-evaluations that suggest a child is easily discouraged and lacks confidence in their social, educational, or other abilities.

The Children in Care Study (CICS)

The CICS was a longitudinal study of the mental health of children in court-ordered foster and kinship care in the Australian state of New South Wales (NSW), carried out between 1997 and 2012. The CICS pilot study was carried out in 1997; the baseline survey was carried out between 2000 and 2003; and a follow-up survey and a parallel adolescent survey were completed between 2010 and 2012. The various surveys obtained foster-parent-reported mental health estimates for children in care, as well as concurrent and retrospective measures of their exposure to potential risk and protective factors. Data were collected from a mail-out questionnaire completed by foster parents and kinship carers, and from the state child welfare and alternative care database. Children were not active participants in the survey.

Study participants

The sampling frame for the CICS cohort was all 4- to 9-year-old children residing in court-ordered foster or kinship care in

NSW, under the guardianship of the Minister. The sampling frame was differentiated from children residing in temporary care without a court order, and from children with custody orders whose parents retained guardianship rights. The sampling frame excluded children in the care of private fostering agencies because it was not practical to enter into separate research agreements with each agency. A 100% sampling procedure was employed, with the proviso that caregivers' contact details could be confirmed via either the electoral roll or a telephone listing. This was necessary because piloting had revealed that caregiver details were not regularly updated on the state database. Survey questionnaires were mailed to the caregivers of 621 eligible children for whom contact details could be confirmed. The study sample was 347 children (176 boys, 171 girls), aged 4–11 years, providing a 56% response rate. Comparisons of participant and non-participant children found the latter entered care at a younger age, had less exposure to maltreatment, and were more likely to have spent the larger part of their life with their present caregivers.

Sixty percent of children were 6–8 years old, with a mean age of 7.8 years. The gender of participants was evenly distributed (176 boys, 171 girls). The proportions of children residing in Sydney, other metropolitan NSW (Wollongong, Central Coast, Newcastle), and regional NSW were 35.5%, 16.5%, and 48%, respectively. Ethnicity was not reliably measured and hence is not reported. Numbers of children residing in foster and kinship care were 297 (86%) and 50 (14%), respectively. Fewer than 6% ($n = 20$) of children entered care without known exposure to maltreatment, with 80% experiencing one or more forms of abuse and 78% experiencing neglect. The median number of confirmed notifications of maltreatment for the sample was 3, the mean time between the first confirmed notification and entry into care was 1.7 years, and the mean age at entry into care was 3.5 years.

Mental health measures

Children's mental health, socialization, and self-esteem were estimated from foster and kinship parent responses on the CBCL and either the ACC (baseline survey) or ACA (follow-up and adolescent surveys). These were incorporated in the mail-out survey questionnaires sent to participant caregivers. The CBCL measures child problem behaviour across eight empirically derived clinical sub-scales, with two 'higher order' scales approximating spectrums of depressive/anxious symptoms ("internalizing") and disruptive behavioural symptoms ("externalizing"; Achenbach & Rescorla, 2001).

Study factors

A large number of potential risk and protective factors were measured retrospectively, concurrently, and prospectively in the baseline and follow-up surveys (Tarren-Sweeney, 2008b). Factors pertaining to children's development, education, and present status (e.g. type and makeup of present placement, recent life events) were measured from a caregiver questionnaire. Various other data were measured retrospectively and prospectively from the state child welfare and alternative care database (e.g. maltreatment history, care history, and birth family factors). Because historical events were mostly recorded on the database shortly after they occurred, these data are thought to be more reliable than those typically obtained in a retrospective design. Essentially, the study sought to measure every factor that might be reliably obtained from the two data sources and which might have some influence on children's mental health.

Abnormal responses to pain

Over several decades of working with children in care, caregivers have often told me that their foster child shows little or no sign of pain following accidents or injuries. This is not limited to instances when a child is emotionally aroused, such as when they are fighting with another child. These children's responses to injury seem different to that of the stoic child, who shows some initial recognition of pain, but then grits her teeth and suffers in silence. On several occasions I have witnessed such behaviour among children that I am assessing, while colleagues sometimes refer to abnormal pain responses in clinical assessment reports and case presentations of children in care.

Pain arises through interactions of physiologic, genetic, and psychosocial mechanisms (Cheng, Foster, & Hester, 2003). The pain experience is generated within a complex neural network, of which sensory neural inputs are but one component (Melzack, 1999). While neural pain pathways are programmed by genetics and sensory conditions, they are further shaped by subjective interpretation of pain-inducing events as well as one's emotional state and stress-regulation systems (Melzack, 1999). The experience of pain thus shapes children's subsequent pain experiences (Cheng et al., 2003). For example, neonates exposed to repeated painful interventions undergo neuroplastic alteration of central pain pathways (Woolf & Salter, 2000), resulting in higher sensitivity to pain during childhood and adolescence (Hermann, Hohmeister, Demirakca, Zohsel, & Flor, 2006).

Behavioural responses to pain need not equate to felt experience. Pain responses that appear abnormal to caregivers may in some cases reflect very high or low pain tolerance, or failure to effectively communicate felt pain. Children at large show sizeable variation in pain tolerance – that is the level of pain they are able or willing to tolerate (Demyttenaere, Finley, Johnston, & McGrath, 2001). Children with high pain tolerance include those who are characteristically stoic and those who show situation-specific endurance (e.g. in the company of peers, on the sports field, or when they know the pain will be brief).

With this in mind, the term abnormal pain response (APR) is used to describe any observable behaviour or self-reported experience suggestive of abnormal experiences, tolerance, or communication of pain. The CICS baseline survey provided the first empirical support for the existence of APR among children residing in long-term alternative care with maltreatment histories, as well as an estimation of the prevalence of this phenomenon among such children. APR was empirically validated in the ACC factor analysis but not in the ACA factor analysis.

Among 347 children surveyed in the CICS, 8.6% were reported with elevated or clinical-range APR scores. Importantly, these children had a high level of corresponding mental health difficulties as measured by other ACC and CBCL scales. In other words, among this study sample APR rarely occurred in isolation from other mental health problems. Almost all of these children had a global mental disorder, as defined by CBCL or ACC total scores in the clinical range.

Eating problems

Clinical assessments of children in foster and kinship care also describe patterns of aberrant eating and food-related behaviour, characterized by excessive eating and drinking and food maintenance (hoarding, storing, stealing, etc.), with or without concurrent obesity. Food is not always stored with the intention of being eaten. Indeed, some children hide or store food indefinitely, despite knowing it will spoil. This pattern resembles the behavioural correlates of hyperphagic short stature (HSS), a form of psychosocial growth failure occurring in children older than 2 years (Skuse, Albanese, Stanhope, Gilmour, & Voss, 1996). HSS is thought to be determined by acute pathogenic or stressful parental care (Green, Campbell, & David, 1984). It describes children with a normal body mass index who display aberrant eating behaviours, especially hyperphagia and polydipsia. An often reported feature of HSS is rapid and spontaneous recovery in alternate care, as evidenced by reversible growth hormone deficiency, 'catch-up' growth, and reduction in aberrant eating behaviour (Green et al., 1984; Powell, Brasel, & Blizzard, 1967). However, there is also evidence that some children fail to spontaneously recover in care (de Kerdanet, Seveno, & Lecornu, 1993). Whereas maltreated growth-delayed children typically attain 'catch up' growth in their first year in foster care (Oliván, 2003), a sizeable minority show static or declining growth velocity (Taitz & King, 1988; Wyatt, Simms, & Horwitz, 1997).

Clinical assessments also occasionally describe school-aged children in foster or residential care who eat or drink from unhealthy sources (e.g. eat from garbage, drink from a toilet or pet bowl) or engage in pica. The latter is not surprising, given that pica is mostly observed among children and adults with developmental disabilities (Stiegler, 2005), and rates of intellectual and language disability among children in care are well in excess of that found among children at large (Halfon, Mendonca, & Berkowitz, 1995; Klee, Kronstadt, & Zlotnick, 1997).

Children in care may also be at risk of more conventional eating problems in adolescence, given their early exposure to maltreatment.

Self-reported emotional abuse in childhood (but not other forms of maltreatment) independently predicted unhealthy eating attitudes in a community sample of 236 adult women (Kent, Waller, & Dagnan, 1999). Another study found that most adults with binge eating disorder recall some history of child abuse or neglect (Grilo & Masheb, 2001). Notwithstanding some negative findings, there is also reasonable evidence of associations between adult eating problems and child sexual and physical abuse (Molinari, 2001). Retrospective studies of the effects of child maltreatment often fail to account for exposure to multiple risk factors that correlate with abuse, such as emotional deprivation and loss. Nonetheless, it is plausible that social learning, attachment, and trauma-related mechanisms account for a higher prevalence of eating problems among adolescent and adult survivors of child maltreatment.

Eating problems measured in the Children in Care Study

Two distinct patterns of eating problems were identified in the CICS from scores on the ACC (Tarren-Sweeney, 2006). The first describes a pattern of excessive eating and the acquisition and retention of food, which has been termed *food maintenance syndrome*. This pattern resembles the behavioural correlates of HSS. The second is a pattern of *pica-type behaviours* that correlates with self-injury and developmental disabilities. A quarter of children displayed clinically significant eating problems, and this rate did not vary by age or gender. The distributions of scores on the food maintenance scale and pica-type index are listed in Table 1.1.

Obesity and overeating were also estimated in the CICS from CBCL items that refer to these problems. Non-obese children (n = 320, 92%) were defined as having a CBCL 'overweight' item score of zero, while obese children (n = 7) were defined by a score of '2' (i.e. overweight = 'very true'). Children scoring '1' (i.e. overweight = 'somewhat true') were considered neither obese nor non-obese (n = 20). Compared to normative and clinic-referred samples at large (Achenbach, 1991), the CICS foster care sample were reported with low prevalence of obesity against high prevalence of overeating, with the greatest discrepancy being observed among boys.

Table 1.1 Distribution of ACC *food maintenance* and *pica-type* scores (*n* = 347)

Scale (max score)	Mean (SD)	Proportion (%) in nominal range		
		Normal	Borderline	Clinical
1. Food maintenance scale (8)[a]		0–2	3–4	5+
Boys	1.2 (1.9)	82	9	9
Girls	1.1 (2.0)	84	6	10
2. Pica-type index (6)[b]		0	1	2+
Boys	0.3 (0.8)	87	7	6
Girls	0.2 (0.7)	87	9	3

a ACC *food maintenance* scale, contains four items: *eats too much, gorges food, hides or stores food, steals food.*
b Nominal ACC *pica-type* index, contains three items: *eats from garbage, eats things that are not food, unhealthy drinking.*

The results from the CICS revealed a distinction between excessive eating and related food maintenance behaviours and the more bizarre pica-type eating problems. These patterns are also associated with different developmental profiles. Whereas both patterns present with co-occurring psychopathology and developmental disabilities, food maintenance behaviour is more consistently aligned with comorbid psychiatric disturbances (particularly disruptive behaviour and affective problems), while pica-type behaviour is more closely associated with reported developmental problems (namely intellectual disability, speech problems, and reading difficulties).

The present findings thus support the validity of two distinct forms of eating disturbance among children in alternative care, which I have termed *food maintenance syndrome* and *pica-type cluster*. Children with food maintenance syndrome show a pattern of excessive eating and food acquisition that appears to be primarily triggered by acute stress (notably maltreatment in care), and which resembles the behavioural correlates of hyperphagic short stature. The pica-type cluster was found to be strongly associated with developmental disabilities and is moderately correlated with self-injury. Both patterns are components of complex and multi-faceted psychopathology, yet neither pattern is associated with the primary predictors of comorbid problems (exposure to early maltreatment and deprivation, and older age at entry into care).

While non-obese hyperphagia has been noted previously among children in care, it is surprising that problems of this magnitude have attracted such little research or clinical attention. It is possible that clinicians have failed to query aberrant eating behaviours among children with normal stature. Importantly, most children with eating problems were reportedly not overweight. Although excessive eating was closely associated with obesity, three quarters of children with food maintenance problems were not obese.

These findings have several implications for clinicians assisting children in care. First, there is a need for assessment of eating and food-related problems in clinical evaluations, and where possible, to track the course of such behaviour (especially across multiple placements). Second, these children should have routine paediatric screening and regular measurement of linear growth velocity, especially if they manifest a pattern of excessive eating and food maintenance behaviour, while having normal body mass index. Finally, the presence of such behaviour in the absence of obesity should alert clinicians to the possibility that a child is encountering abuse or deprivation in care (especially emotional abuse, such as scapegoating or rejection) or other major stressors. It should be emphasized, however, that the presence of such behaviours does not confirm pathogenic foster care. In other words, abuse in care should not be diagnosed from children's eating and food-related behaviour.

Sexual behaviour problems (SBP)

A recent taskforce defined SBP among pre-adolescent children as sexual behaviour that is developmentally inappropriate (e.g. age inappropriate) or potentially harmful to the self or others (Chaffin et al., 2008). This includes behaviour of a sexual nature that infringes on the rights of others (such as use of coercion or force), and that which is indicative of emotional distress (Silovsky & Niec, 2002). The task of identifying what child sexual behaviours are atypical or maladaptive SBP is aided by a body of research that has established normative (i.e. developmentally typical) child sexual behaviour within age and gender groupings, using standardized measures such as the Child Sexual Behavior Inventory

(Friedrich, Fisher, Broughton, Houston, & Shafran, 1998; Friedrich & Grambsch, 1992). Among children at large, the frequency of caregiver-reported sexual behaviours peaks at around age 5, after which it steadily declines throughout childhood before re-emerging in adolescence. Normative sexual behaviour, especially in early childhood, consists mainly of self-stimulating behaviours, exposing private parts, and intrusion of personal boundaries (Friedrich et al., 1998). Conversely, intrusive or coercive sexual behaviour is uncommon among children at large.

What accounts for child sexual behaviour problems?

Early studies of sexually offending youth found that coercive sexual behaviour was strongly correlated with sexual and physical abuse as well as with broader indicators of family dysfunction (Fehrenbach, Smith, Montastersky, & Deisher, 1986; Kahn & Lafond, 1988). However, the developmental pathways of such youth may differ to that of children and young people with SBP who do not proceed to sexual offending. A number of contemporary studies have identified social experiences that predict sexual behaviour problems among children and young people without reference to offending status (Adams & McClellan, 1995; Friedrich, 2005; Friedrich, Davies, Feher, & Wright, 2003; Gray, Pithers, Busconi, & Houchens, 1999; Letourneau, Schoenwald, & Sheidow, 2004; Silovsky & Niec, 2002). The most important of these predictors is child sexual abuse (CSA). A strong link between CSA and SBP has been found in studies of:

1   Maltreated children (Cosentino, Meyer-Bahlburg, Alpert, Weinberg, & Gaines, 1995; Friedrich et al., 2001; Friedrich & Grambsch, 1992; Mian, Marton, & LeBaron, 1996; White, Halpin, Strom, & Santilli, 1988);
2   Adolescent sexual offenders (Burton, 2000);
3   Children and young people referred to clinical services (Adams & McClellan, 1995);
4   Children at large (Friedrich et al., 2003).

The specificity of the relationship between SBP and CSA has been a major focus of research with particular reference to the reliability of SBP as a marker for CSA (Drach, Wientzen, & Ricci, 2001). There is some evidence that CSA influences sexual behaviour and sexual relationships into adulthood (Paolucci, Genuis, & Violato, 2001). Several reviews have concluded that CSA is specifically harmful to children's mental health, relationship capacity, and sexual development (Kendall-Tackett, Williams, & Finkelhor, 1993; Putnam, 2003; World Health Organization, 2002). Yet CSA was found to predict *only a moderate proportion* of the variance in SBP among a large population sample (Friedrich et al., 2003). Given the secrecy surrounding CSA, it is difficult to obtain valid estimates of children's exposure. If there is a direct and strong relationship between CSA and SBP, then research estimates of the effect size will be diluted by undetected CSA (Friedrich, Trane, & Gully, 2005; Ricci, Drach, & Wientzen, 2005).

Other identified correlates of SBP can be construed under broad categories of *child maltreatment, indicators of family dysfunction and parenting difficulties, developmental difficulties*, and *age-inappropriate exposure to sexually explicit behaviour and knowledge*. Beyond CSA, the most cited maltreatment correlate of SBP is *physical abuse* (Friedrich et al., 2003; Gray et al., 1999; Letourneau et al., 2004; Silovsky & Niec, 2002). There is evidence of a relationship between physical abuse and the development of coercive/aggressive sexual offending behaviour (Becker, 1998; Benoit & Kennedy, 1992). However, not all SBP is coercive, and research designs rarely control for potential confounders of physical abuse (including CSA). In a study that did control for several key confounders, physical abuse independently predicted SBP (Friedrich et al., 2003). SBP is also associated with early age-inappropriate exposure to sexual behaviour or knowledge, such as witnessing parental sex and pornography (Friedrich et al., 2003).

The ACC sexual behaviour scale

Why was the ACC designed to measure problematic sexual behaviour? First it was realized that the CBCL's five sexual behaviour items do not adequately describe the range of SBP observed among children in alternative care. A second consideration was a need to restrict the length of the CICS survey questionnaire so as not to overwhelm potential respondents. This ruled against using an additional instrument to measure sexual behaviour, such as the Child Sexual Behavior Inventory (CSBI; Friedrich, 1997), or the Child Sexual Behavior Checklist (CSBCL; Johnson, 1993). The results of a U.S. normative study of child sexual behaviour, using the CSBI, helped identify normative behaviours that should be excluded from the ACC (Friedrich et al., 1998). Fifteen nominal SBP items were written for a 132-item research version of the ACC. Following item and factor analyses, nine items were allocated to a SBP sub-scale, one item was assigned to another sub-scale, two items were retained as 'other items', and three items were discarded.

What was learned about child sexual behaviour problems in the Children in Care Study?

About a third of children were reported as having some sexual behaviour problems. Girls had significantly higher SBP scores than boys. There was moderate correlation of the sexual behaviour scale with ACC scores measuring various types of interpersonal/attachment difficulties, as well as with the CBCL externalizing sub-scales. The proportions of children with SBP scores above 2 ($n = 57$) having total CBCL and ACC scores in the clinical range were 89% and 93%, respectively. Factors that were strongly associated with SBP scores included children's *age at entry into care*, their estimated *length of time exposed to maltreatment*, the ratio of *time in present placement/time in care* (a measure of placement stability), several measures of care status and permanency, and having known exposure to contact sexual abuse. Some notable factors that were not associated with SBP scores were *type of care* (kinship vs. foster care), *reported intellectual disability, non-contact sexual abuse*, and most other forms of abuse and neglect, including *physical abuse* and *witnessing parental violence*.

Independent predictors of ACC sexual behaviour problems

The Children in Care Study identified concurrent and retrospectively measured correlates of SBP from a large number of potential risk factors. Independent predictors of clinically meaningful SBP were identified in a two-step hierarchical logistic regression model. Further to the two-step hierarchical logistic regression model, a three-step analysis was conducted to explore relationships between sexual behaviour and scales that are suggestive of attachment difficulties, while controlling for potential confounders. The analysis for the aggregate sample identified four independent predictors of SBP scores above 2, namely *older age at entry into care* (O.R. = 1.4, p = 0.001), *contact sexual abuse* (O.R. = 3.9, p = 0.002), *female gender* (O.R. = 2.0, p = 0.04), and *lower ratio of time in present placement/time in care* (a measure of placement stability) (O.R. = 0.34, p = 0.05). The exploratory three-step logistic regression, which added three ACC attachment-related scale scores (*Pseudomature, Non-reciprocal*, and *Indiscriminate*), accounted for an additional 25% of the dichotomous score variance (i.e. 45% in total). This model suggests that moderate associations between SBP and Non-reciprocal and Indiscriminate interpersonal behaviour problems are independent of other variables.

Possible mechanisms for development of sexual behaviour problems among children in care

Gender

In the CICS there were large gender differences in item score distributions, with girls scoring more often than boys on seven of the nine SBP sub-scale items. Girls had significantly higher average scores than boys (1.6 vs. 0.9). The finding that girls in this high-risk pre-adolescent sample had higher SBP scores than boys was intriguing. Friedrich et al. (2003) did not find a gender effect in their normative study of pre-adolescent SBP. The CICS result seems consistent with the higher reported incidence of contact sexual abuse among subject girls (McClellan et al., 1997). However, female gender strongly predicted SBP scores, even after controlling for sexual abuse. SBP among high-risk girls might possibly be linked to acculturation and attachment development in the face of severe deprivation and abuse. Boys and girls also presented with different patterns of disturbance in interpersonal behaviour (Tarren-Sweeney & Hazell, 2006). The CICS data suggest that, given similar early adverse experiences, boys in care are more likely to develop emotionally withdrawn, inhibited attachment responses and abnormal responses to pain, while girls are more likely to develop controlling, pseudomature attachment behaviour and sexual behaviour problems (Tarren-Sweeney & Hazell, 2006). An alternative explanation is that the ACC could be biased towards measurement of SBP that is more commonly manifested by girls while failing to measure sexual behaviours that are more commonly reported among boys (such as aggressive sexual behaviours).

Cumulative exposure to adversity

In the CICS, *age at entry into care* was a strong independent pre-care predictor of children's SBP scores, as it was of mental health in general (Tarren-Sweeney, 2008b). For chronically deprived and maltreated children, their age at entry into care provides an approximation of their length of exposure to adversity. This does not imply that all children endured chronic maltreatment and deprivation from birth. However, the child protection histories of subject children suggest the vast majority resided in dysfunctional family environments for most of their pre-care lives. It should be remembered that these children represent the most seriously and chronically maltreated children in the state.

Whereas a single harmful event may have life-altering consequences for children at large, the impact of individual events is tempered among children exposed to chronic and multiple adversities. A number of researchers have reported that broad indicators of exposure to maltreatment, family conflict, and other psychosocial risk factors account for a greater proportion of the variance in children's mental health than exposure to specific types or single instances of harm (Fergusson & Lynskey, 1996; Rutter, 1999). The CICS findings suggest this may also be true for SBP. Aside from contact sexual abuse, no specific form of abuse or neglect predicted children's SBP. Indeed, the only other maltreatment-related variable associated with children's SBP continuous scores was the time between their first confirmed notification and their entry into care, which is perhaps a crude indicator of cumulative exposure to adversity. Furthermore, several factors previously identified as correlates of SBP were not associated with SBP scores in the CICS sample, notably physical abuse and witnessing parental violence.

At first glance, the positive correlation between age and SBP scores found in the CICS contradicts prior findings that sexual behaviour is more conspicuous among younger pre-adolescent children (Bonner & Walker, 1999; Friedrich et al., 2003; Friedrich et al., 2001). However, the CICS age effect is probably illusory, accounted for by children's age at entry into care. Older children were more likely to have entered care later, with greater cumulative exposure to adversity. Similarly, the moderate recency effect found in the relationship between contact sexual abuse and problematic sexual behaviour was at least partially confounded by children's age at entry into care. Although children who were sexually abused before age 3 showed almost no SBP, they mostly entered care shortly after the abuse occurred.

An alternative explanation for these findings would be afforded by a higher rate of undetected sexual abuse among 'late arrivers' into care. Although the rate of undetected abuse cannot be estimated, the rate of confirmed sexual abuse (12%) was rather low for such a high-risk population. My own clinical experience is that children in care often first disclose pre-care sexual abuse many years after entering care.

Attachment difficulties and sexual behaviour problems

Aside from sexual behaviour, SBP has a strong interpersonal dimension, reflecting maladaptive socialization. Children in care are particularly prone to poor socialization and relationship disturbances in the wake of early attachment difficulties (Fonagy, 2003; Howe & Fearnley, 2003; Minnis, Everett, Pelosi, Dunn, & Knapp, 2006; O'Connor & Rutter, 2000). As mentioned earlier in this chapter, Friedrich (2007) theorized that attachment difficulties underlie the development of SBP. Although his attachment-focussed intervention was based on this premise, there has been a lack of data to support this theory. However, the CICS findings provide some empirical support for a proximal relationship between attachment and SBP. Children's SBP scores correlated strongly (around $r = 0.50$) with ACC sub-scales measuring pseudomature, non-reciprocal, and indiscriminate interpersonal behaviour. Furthermore, logistic regression modelling suggests these close relationships are not confounded by other factors. Although it remains uncertain as to how closely these scales reflect either attachment insecurity or attachment disorder behaviours, at this point it is useful to consider some possible mechanisms linking attachment difficulties to the development of SBP. It should be emphasized that the following discussion is speculative, referring to generated rather than tested hypotheses.

The non-reciprocal sub-scale measures an avoidant, disengaged, and non-empathic relationship style. It is speculated that high scores on this scale approximate the inhibited form of DSM-IV reactive attachment disorder (American Psychiatric Association, 2000), which possibly represents a severe manifestation of attachment disorganization (Howe, 2003; van IJzendoorn & Bakermans-Kranenburg, 2003). This scale correlates moderately with CBCL rule-breaking behaviour and SBP. These findings suggest that low empathy in the context of attachment disturbance may contribute to the development of SBP among high-risk children.

The indiscriminate sub-scale measures over-familiarity and absence of discrimination and personal boundaries in social relationships, which parallels a disturbance of non-attachment commonly observed among emotionally deprived children (O'Connor et al., 1999). It is speculated that high scores on this scale approximate the disinhibited form of DSM-IV reactive attachment disorder as well as the proposed DSM-5 disinhibited social engagement disorder. It is not inconceivable that this type of attachment disturbance could be manifested as sexualized indiscriminate affection. We might also speculate whether, in the absence of meaningful attachments, such children might have difficulty in discriminating between non-sexual and sexualized affection. This might be especially so if they have been sexually abused.

The pseudomature sub-scale measures a pattern of aberrant interpersonal behaviour marked by precocious pseudomaturity and controlling behaviour, and an element of parent–child role-reversal. It has been suggested that this pattern represents an additional form of attachment disturbance (Lieberman & Zeanah, 1995), or using alternative conceptualization, a maladaptive attachment strategy (e.g. Type A5–6 of the dynamic-maturational model; Crittenden, 2006). Pseudomaturity and associated role reversal have been previously linked to SBP (White et al., 1988). Much SBP is problematic because it is highly age inappropriate. The behaviour is deviant because it is developmentally harmful for the child. Yet precocious, pseudomature children attempt to maintain an adult lifestyle. This might in some instances be precipitated or facilitated by sexual abuse by an adult or by family conditions in which the child assumes responsibility for the care of their parents and/or siblings (role reversal). The pseudomature profile also entails controlling behaviours consistent with intrusive SBP. It can thus be hypothesized that precocious pseudomaturity represents one pathway to SBP among children with attachment difficulties. However, the CICS findings provide only limited support for this hypothesis. The pseudomature sub-scale score did not independently predict SBP, suggesting it was confounded by other variables.

Attachment–related difficulties and felt insecurity

Attachment–related difficulties of children in alternative care

A high prevalence of social and interpersonal relationship difficulties was found among children and young people in the CICS. The findings suggest such difficulties are a hallmark feature of the clinical presentations of many children and young people in foster care. Inhibited and disinhibited forms of attachment disturbance were hypothesized during the development of the ACC, and scales that broadly refer to these phenomena ('non-reciprocal' and 'indiscriminate' interpersonal behaviour) were derived through factor analysis. It is likely that high scores on these scales represent, in most instances, socially determined attachment-related disturbances, because sample scores on these scales were strongly predicted by children's exposure to social adversity and their age at entry into care (Tarren-Sweeney, 2008b). Nonetheless, one should be mindful that social relatedness problems among children in care may in some instances be determined more by brain injury, intellectual disability, autism spectrum disorders, or temperament (Richters & Volkmar, 1994). The author has also observed cases in which non-reciprocal interpersonal behaviour is situation specific. For example, these difficulties may be apparent in a child's relationship with their foster parents but not with their birth parents. The emergence of the 'pseudomature' factor had not been anticipated. This pattern of interpersonal behaviour has been described previously (Lieberman & Zeanah, 1995), but is not presently thought of as an attachment-related clinical phenomenon.

Inhibited and disinhibited attachment disorder behaviours are presently conceptualized in DSM-5 as reactive attachment disorder (RAD; representing the inhibited form) and disinhibited social engagement disorder (the disinhibited form). It has been suggested these sub-types may not be symptomatically distinct (Minnis & Keck, 2003; Smyke, Dumitrescu, & Zeanah, 2002), and an alternative classification of infant mental health disorders (the Diagnostic Classification: 0–3R) includes a mixed pattern of inhibition and disinhibition (Zero to Three, 2005). Among the CICS sample, there was moderate to high correlations of scores on the pseudomature, non-reciprocal, indiscriminate, and insecure scales. A number of ACC-CBCL symptom profiles derived through cluster analyses (described later in this chapter) include simultaneous high scores on combinations of two to four of those scales. Furthermore, few children were reported with discrete (or *pure*) forms of social or interpersonal relationship difficulties. Together, this suggests that many children in care present with a complex array of attachment-related difficulties that is more correctly conceptualized as individual *profiles* of attachment-related difficulties rather than discrete *types* of attachment disorder.

Felt insecurity in relation to attachment security and trauma-related anxiety

The meaning of high scores on the insecure scale remains somewhat uncertain because the scale does not delineate between state and trait insecurity. Insecure and overly conforming behaviours may indicate an insecure attachment style, but may equally represent a child's adaptation to previous losses (including foster placement breakdowns). Furthermore, there are likely to be many and varied systemic pressures affecting the felt security of children in care. The CICS provided several insights into the characteristics and patterns of felt insecurity and emotional difficulties experienced by children in care. Although the ACC *insecure* and *anxious-distrustful* scales appear to respectively measure felt security and trauma-related anxiety, they correlated highly with the CBCL *anxious-depressed* and *withdrawn-depressed* sub-scales, and with the DSM-oriented *affective problems* and *anxiety problems* scales. However, all but one of the ACC-CBCL symptom profiles derived through cluster analyses (described later in this chapter) were characterized by relatively low DSM-oriented affective problems and anxiety problems and ACC anxious-distrustful behaviours. This was somewhat unexpected given the extent of social adversity and developmental trauma that children experience before entering care. The present findings point to the possibility that anxiety among children in care tends to be more strongly experienced as a component of felt insecurity (i.e. as measured by the ACC insecure scale).

Complex attachment- and trauma-related difficulties

For children in care, there are big question marks around the coherence and validity of clinical assessments that attempt to frame complex attachment- and trauma-related symptomatology within standard psychiatric diagnoses (De Jong, 2010). During the development of the ACC, a large number of clinical assessment reports written for children in alternative care were reviewed. Most of these reports were written by psychologists and psychiatrists working in specialist public health services, child welfare and alternate care agencies, and private practice. Typically, such children have several assessment reports on their case files. The review identified considerable disagreement between the assessors about children's mental health diagnoses, as well as a tendency to frame complex psychopathology as a series of discrete, comorbid disorders. At its simplest, patterns and complexity of children's psychiatric symptoms can be construed in terms of *comorbidity*: the co-occurrence of various combinations of dichotomous psychiatric disorders. There are several common, well-observed comorbid presentations (e.g. attention-deficit hyperactivity disorder; ADHD with co-occurring oppositional-defiant disorder, or ODD; and comorbid mood and anxiety disorders). However, constructing more complex symptomatology as a series of comorbid diagnoses holds less conceptual validity.

Symptom profile types

One empirical method for investigating symptom patterns and complexity is to construct *symptom profiles*, which are graphical representations of the presence (e.g. in terms of prevalence, frequency, and/or severity) of any number of symptom constructs – either as continuously distributed scores or on multi-level dimensional scales. Derived using cluster analysis, these profiles provide a means for examining the construct validity of existing taxonomies, and for proposing alternative taxonomies. Some years ago I derived a set of symptom profiles for the CICS child sample ($N = 347$). Gender-specific cluster analyses were performed across six ACC scales (Sexual behaviour, Pseudomature interpersonal behaviour, Non-reciprocal interpersonal behaviour, Indiscriminate interpersonal behaviour, Insecure, and Anxious-distrustful) and five CBCL DSM-oriented scales (Affective problems, Anxiety problems, Attention-deficit/hyperactivity problems, Oppositional defiant problems, and Conduct problems).

Symptom profile types were drawn for each of the boy and girl symptom clusters, with mean cluster scores placed on a four-range severity scale. For the DSM-oriented scales, the four ranges were defined as *normative* (*T*-scores < 63, representing scores that are clearly normative); *elevated* (*T*-scores = 63–69, representing sub-clinical scores that are less clearly normative, with the upper end encompassing the CBCL borderline clinical range); *clinically indicated* (*T*-scores = 70–73, the moderate end of the clinical range); and *marked clinical* (*T*-scores > 73, the severe end of the clinical range). For the ACC scales, existing cut-points delineating between the *normative* and *elevated* ranges and between the *elevated* and *clinical* ranges were utilized. Given a relative lack of research on the clinical meaning of high ACC scale scores, it was reasoned that assignment of scores to a *marked clinical* range should be conservative. Consequently, in comparison with the CBCL scales, greater proportions of the ACC score ranges were defined within the *clinically indicated* range, and lesser proportions within the *marked clinical* range. The derived symptom profiles are shown in Figure 1.2.

Both the boy and girl symptom profile types are delineated more by elevation than shape. Only a few of the profiles point to discrete, non-complex disorders. Profile #1 describes normative behaviour

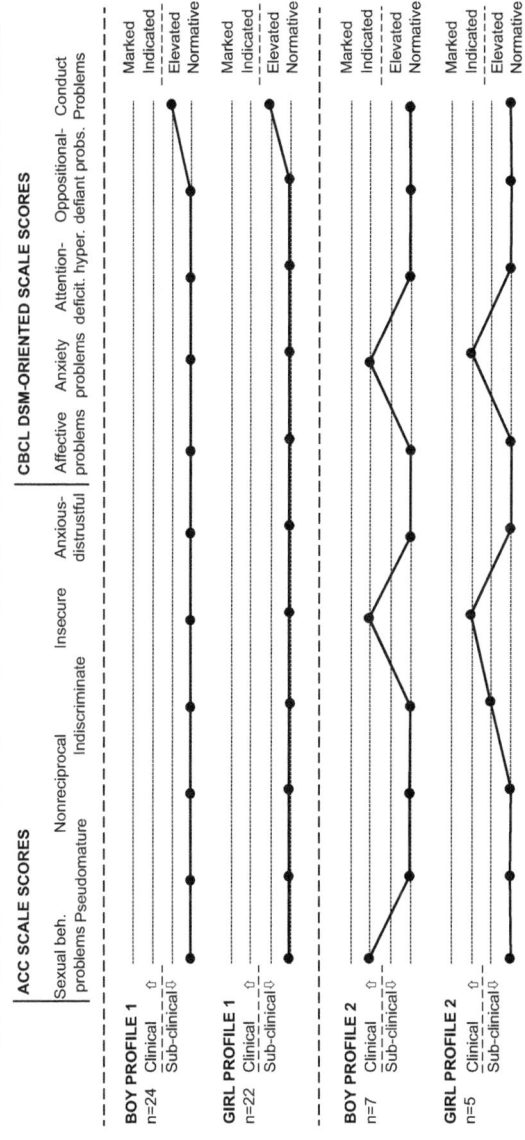

Figure 1.2 Symptom profile types derived from cluster analyses of ACC and CBCL DSM-oriented scale scores

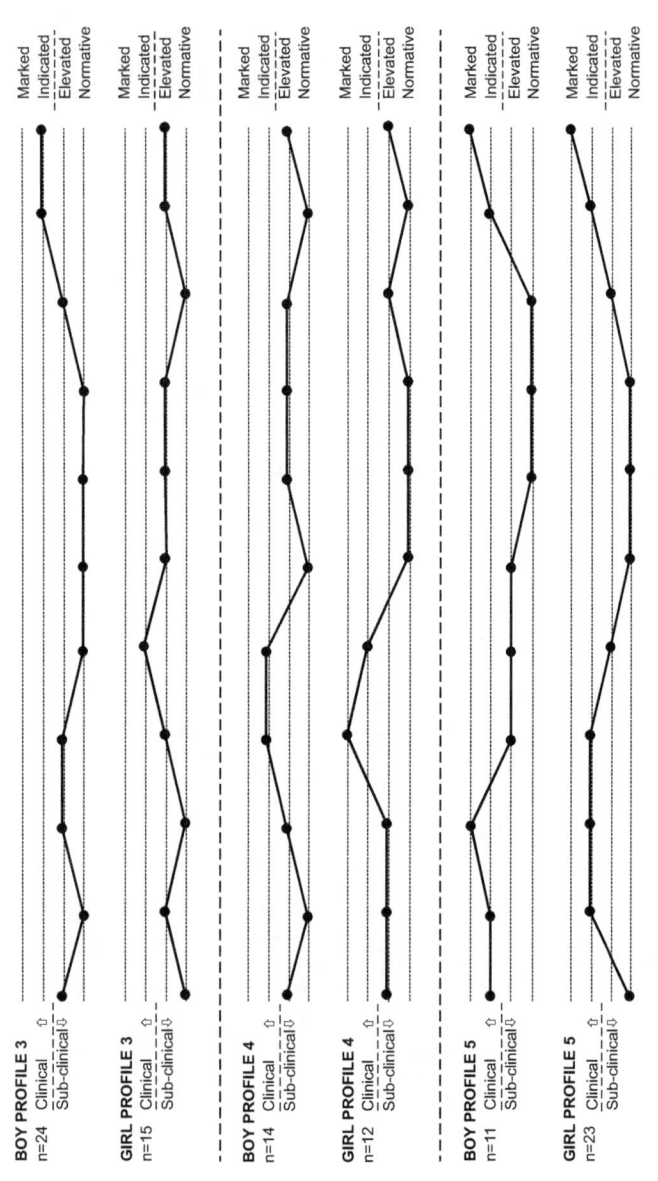

Figure 1.2 (Continued)

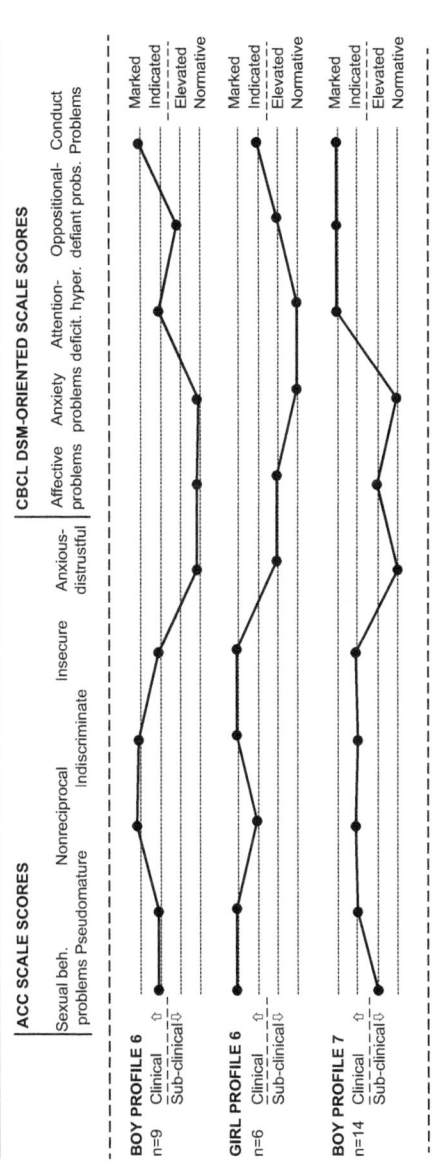

Figure 1.2 (Continued)

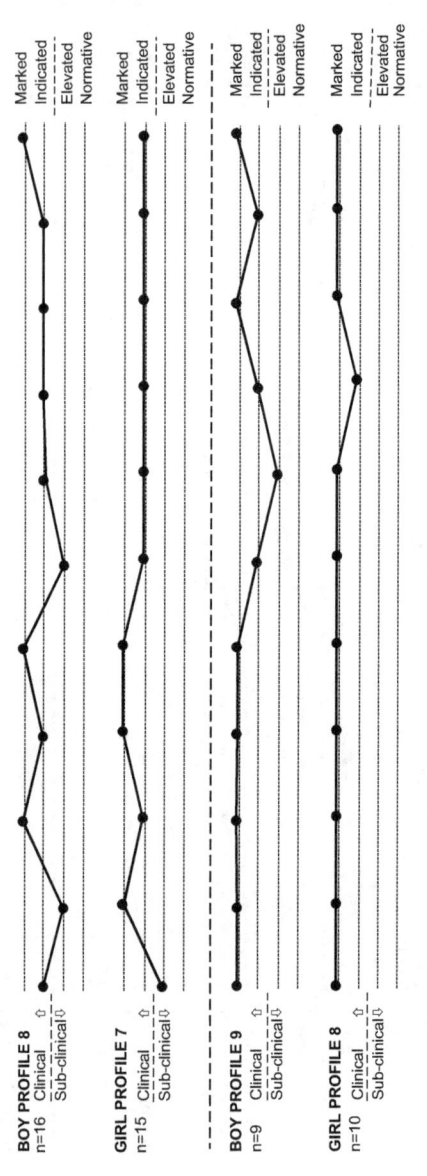

Figure 1.2 (Continued)

with elevated, sub-clinical conduct problems. Profile #2 represents an *anxious-insecure* type for girls, and an *anxious-insecure-sexual problems* type for boys, both of which are fairly specific to these symptoms. Boy profile #3 is a relatively simple *conduct/oppositional-defiant* type. However, the other profile types reveal varying degrees of symptom complexity. Girl profile #3 and boy profile #4 consist of one or two clinical-level scores combined with elevated sub-clinical difficulties across most of the remaining scales. Boy profile #5 and girl profile #5 are more complex externalizing types, characterized by co-occurring interpersonal difficulties (as well as sexual behaviour problems for girls). While the #5 profiles are possibly 'accommodated' within present DSM and ICD classifications, the #6, #7, and #8 profiles and boy profile #9 all describe complex symptom patterns that are inadequately conceptualized within present nosology.

Complex symptomatology that is inadequately conceptualized within DSM and ICD

The cluster analyses of ACC and CBCL DSM-oriented scale scores revealed that 30% of children were reported with normative difficulties; another 15% had elevated, sub-clinical checklist scores; and around 35% had relatively non-complex, clinically significant psychopathology that can be conceptualized as discrete mental disorders or comorbidity within standard classification systems. *The remaining 20% of subject children were reported with complex and severe symptomatology that is not adequately conceptualized within DSM and ICD classifications of mental disorders.*

The presence of hallmark social and interpersonal relationship difficulties among a large proportion of children in care, which overlays and possibly mediates children's experience of other types of symptoms, adds to symptom complexity. This complexity accounts for some surprising results. Despite a high prevalence of clinical-level DSM-oriented attention-deficit/hyperactivity scores among the present sample (Tarren-Sweeney & Hazell, 2006), an ADHD profile type was not located for either gender. Instead, the findings suggest that clinically significant inattention/over-activity is largely manifested as a component of complex symptomatology that includes social impairments. Similarly, a lack of symptom specificity precluded the presence of the CBCL dysregulation profile among the CICS sample.

The psychopathology described by the most complex and elevated symptom profiles mirrors somewhat the diagnostic criteria and clinical presentations of Bessel van der Kolk and colleagues' proposed developmental trauma disorder (DTD) (D'Andrea, Ford, Stolbach, Spinazzola, & van der Kolk, 2012; van der Kolk, 2005). Notably, the present study sample had almost universal exposure to severe and chronic social adversity and trauma prior to their entry into care. The present findings partially support the rationale for introducing DTD or a similar construct into DSM and ICD classification systems, in that these findings demonstrate that DTD provides a more accurate conceptualization of complex attachment- and trauma-related psychopathology than that provided by existing taxonomies. *However, the present findings caution against thinking of developmental trauma disorder, or complex symptomatology in general, as discrete, symptom-specific, clinical phenomena – suggesting instead the need for a symptom profile approach to clinical formulation.*

No basis for a new taxonomy of complex attachment- and trauma-related disorders

There are some distinct differences between the derived symptom profiles that merit further research, and which suggest new ways of conceptualizing complex attachment- and trauma-related disorders. Beyond this, however, the profiles *do not* provide a basis for a taxonomy of complex attachment- and trauma-related disorders. The clusters are differentiated more by profile elevation than profile shape or pattern, suggesting an absence of *typology*. Furthermore, while the present cluster analyses yielded statistically delineated symptom profile types, their clinical distinctness is questionable. Close inspection of children's individual score profiles shows a lack of clear delineation between the derived profile types and considerable variability between children's symptom profiles. This implies that any taxonomy of complex attachment- and trauma-related disorders is likely to have poor specificity. It may be that much of the symptomatology identified in the CICS is too complex, and shows too much variability across children's individual profiles, to allow for traditional classification.

What causes such complexity and high rates of clinical-level difficulties?

Mental health and resilience among children in statutory care, and those who are subsequently raised under permanent guardianship (such as adoption), arise from complex, time-sensitive interactions between genotype, prenatal conditions, pre-care and in-care psychosocial conditions and events, and infant neurological development (Rutter, 2000). The social experiences that predicate entry into care represent critical developmental risks for their well-being and mental health. Foremost of these is exposure to psychological trauma, emotional deprivation, and other conditions that negate opportunity for secure attachments. Children in alternative care also encounter a number of uncommon developmental events, the most critical being the loss of their biological parents, integration into new families or non-family settings, and (for some at least) unstable placements. Developmental psychopathology models pertaining to maltreated children (Cicchetti, Toth, & Maughan, 2000) and profoundly deprived inter-country adoptees (O'Connor et al., 1999) are thus only partially valid for children in care, as there are both commonalities and differences in their experience. Conversely, there is considerable commonality in the developmental pathways of children raised in long-term foster care and children who are subsequently adopted from care.

Maltreatment and other severe social adversity prior to alternative care

The complex and severe symptom profiles described in the previous section are developmentally based, and thus tend to follow a long-term developmental course. Without improvements in a child's developmental conditions, these more serious attachment- and trauma-related difficulties are likely to become increasingly trait-like, having lifelong implications for social, educational, and occupational functioning. Even with optimal reparative conditions (consistently sensitive and loving care, and unconditional commitment) and with specialized clinical support, children's recovery in alternative care tends to be slow, testing their caregivers' commitment and strength. However, it is important that we keep some perspective on the relative influence of pre-care and within-care adversity on children's developmental pathways. It has often been observed that older children in foster care on average have poorer mental health than younger children. In the past, this was wrongly interpreted as evidence that children's mental health deteriorated in care (see the discussion on age effects earlier in this chapter). There are some children whose mental health does get worse, particularly among those who come into alternative care at older ages with pre-existing mental health difficulties, and who go on to experience serial placement disruptions. However, this age effect is largely illusory. The older a child is when they enter alternative care, the greater the likelihood that they do so with pre-existing developmental difficulties and mental ill health – hence the age effect.

In my Children in Care Study, the strongest predictor of the presence, severity, and complexity of mental health difficulties was a child's *age at entry into care*, with entry at younger ages being protective (Tarren-Sweeney, 2008b). There was a strong, linear relationship that was not confounded by other factors, including genetic and prenatal risk exposures. A child's age when they come into care provides a proxy measure of their length of post-birth exposure to severe social adversity, notably child abuse and neglect. This is consistent with both cumulative trauma exposure models and attachment theory.

Children's experience of legally impermanent statutory care

While growing up in legally impermanent statutory care is preferable to ongoing exposure to maltreatment and other severe social adversity, there is good evidence that it systemically compromises children's development and well-being. Quality of care, caregiver bonding, caregiver commitment, and maltreatment in care are all factors that directly influence children's felt security and psychological development, and regulate their potential to recover from attachment- and trauma-related psychopathology (Tarren-Sweeney, 2008b). Attachment theory predicts that the therapeutic potential of alternative care should vary according to the characteristics of children's attachment systems at entry into care and to caregiver sensitivity and ability to provide a 'secure base' (Bowlby, 1988; Schofield, 2002). Regardless of prior conditions, the attachment systems of infants who enter foster care are found to be responsive to changes in parenting style (Dozier, Stovall, Albus, & Bates, 2001). Beyond infancy, children entering foster care at progressively older ages manifest more interpersonal behaviour problems suggestive of attachment disturbances (Tarren-Sweeney, 2008b). The attachment difficulties of late-placed children are more resistant to therapeutic change in response to markedly improved care. This is partly due to them having more 'established' internal representations of self and others (Milan & Pinderhughes, 2000). We know that caring for children who have these difficulties can be exceedingly difficult and bewildering. More enlightened agencies are becoming aware of the need to modify models of statutory long-term care to facilitate children's attachment to their caregivers (Dozier, Bick, & Bernard, 2011; Schofield, 2002). This is particularly critical for later-placed children, for whom a legally permanent placement may not be possible or desirable. However, I believe that there are good developmental reasons why most children who have an ongoing need for care should not be growing up in statutory care.

The developmental risks children encounter in statutory care are systemically interconnected, involving complex interactions of child welfare practices, caregiver motivation, the child's perceptions of their legal and relational permanence, and their felt security. In many ways, child welfare practices and legal frameworks undermine foster parents' bonding and commitment to their children, and generate felt insecurity among children and their foster parents. Some of this is due to the way the state intrudes into foster family life, and foster parents' lack of power and control. This is perhaps best explained through some examples. In my NSW study, 'caregiver expectation of restoration' independently predicted poorer mental health among pre-adolescent children in care (Tarren-Sweeney, 2008b). Foster parents have told me on a number of occasions that they had been so devastated by the loss of a child to whom they had bonded that they avoided becoming emotionally close to children subsequently placed with them. This was also reported in a U.K. study examining the impact of the state on foster family life (Nutt, 2006). While this strategy is designed to protect foster parents' emotions, it harms children's development. When I first worked in child welfare, the government agency I worked for screened out foster care applicants deemed to be 'adoptive parents in disguise', on the grounds that the children already had parents, and such applicants would not have a 'professional' attitude to restoration. This is possibly fine for children destined to spend a short time in care while awaiting the opportunity to return home. However, many of those rejected applicants brought with them the emotional commitment that children in long-term care need. Another example is that some agencies manage the risk of sexual harm to children in care by banning physical intimacy between the children and their foster parents (Meakings & Selwyn, 2016).

The importance of stability

Placement disruption has particularly harmful consequences for children growing up in alternative care and is all too common in legally impermanent placements. Statutory care placements typically disrupt when foster parents are confronted by severe behavioural difficulties, or when they are not able to cope with (or misinterpret) children's maladaptive attachment behaviours. Placement disruptions in turn cause further deterioration in children's mental health (Delfabbro & Barber, 2003; Newton, Litrownik, & Landsverk, 2000). These bi-directional effects increase the chance of a further disruption. Placement disruptions reinforce the child's distorted and maladaptive representations of themselves as being essentially unlovable, and of parents and other caregivers as being essentially rejecting of them. This accounts for further deterioration in their mental health and social behaviours, such that they subsequently become even more difficult to care for. It accounts for a pattern of serial placement disruptions commonly seen among children in care (especially those who come in to care at older ages). With each successive disruption, the bi-directional effects are amplified, causing a spiralling decline in children's social functioning, and making further placement breakdowns ever more predictable and frequent. I see this phenomenon as a dramatic example of a *developmental cascade*. The developmental conditions necessary for recovery from attachment-related difficulties thus diminish, as do their prospects for being raised by a family. Instead these children and young people mostly transition to residential care. This is why protecting long-term and permanent placements from any disruption is so critical.

Additional related factors that contribute to placement stability are the type of care order, the extent to which those orders infer that the placement is truly permanent (i.e. 'for life'), and the associated caregiver commitment. This is borne out when we compare placement stability rates for various care orders. The United Kingdom provides the best available data for such comparisons. Looking first at children restored to their birth parents, a recent study of neglected children restored from care (n = 138) found that 2 years after restoration 59% had experienced further maltreatment and 50% had been returned to care, while 5 years post-restoration 65% had returned to care (Lutman & Farmer, 2013). A second study that examined census data for children in care (n = 3,872) found similar instability among those children who were restored to their birth parents. One third had returned to care within 6 months, and two thirds had returned to care one or more times within 4 years of the initial restoration (Wade, Biehal, Farrelly, & Sinclair, 2010). The disruption rate for children restored to drug or alcohol abusing parents rose to 81%.

A prospective study of 374 U.K. children in foster care found that 7 or more years after entering their index foster placement, 45% had been adopted, restored to their birth parents, or were being cared for under a residence order (this includes adoptions and residence orders with the former foster parents); 32% remained with their same foster parents; and 23% had one or more placement changes (Biehal, Ellison, Baker, & Sinclair, 2009).

A recent landmark study in England examined the complete national dataset for three types of permanent orders. The five-year disruption rates for these orders were as follows: residence order = 14.7% (147/1,000); special guardianship order = 5.7% (57/1,000); adoption order = 0.7% (7/1,000) (Selwyn et al., 2014). The cumulative disruption rate for adoptions increased to 3.2% after 12 years. The small number of adoption disruptions mostly occurred when the children were teenagers. Conversely, around two thirds of disruptions to special guardianship and residence placements occurred before children turned age 11.

It is possible that the differences in disruption rates for these three types of orders could be accounted for by a selection bias, whereby children who have less risk for disruption (in terms of their developmental difficulties and care histories) are more likely to be adopted, while those with higher risk for disruption are more likely to be placed on residence orders. However, statistical risk modelling of disruptions (Cox regression) confirmed that the type of order is the strongest predictor of disruption, independent of other factors, including age at entry into care and age at permanent placement (Selwyn et al., 2014). Furthermore, both this national study and another recent English survey (DeJong et al., 2016) found that levels and rates of mental health difficulties among samples of adopted children are comparable to that previously estimated for English children in care. Another possible explanation for the low adoption disruption rate is that children adopted by their foster parents already enjoy stable, 'road-tested' placements, where foster parent bonding and commitment are established. However, the Selwyn et al. study found no difference in disruption rates for adoptions by foster parents versus other adoptions. This gives us some confidence in the durability of adoptions by new, unrelated parents.

What proportions of children's mental health improves, deteriorates, or remains much the same?

Cross-sectional surveys have consistently found that older children and young people in statutory care tend to have more difficulties than younger children (Armsden, Pecora, Payne, & Szatkiewicz, 2000; Dubowitz, Zuravin, Starr, Feigelman, & Harrington, 1993; Heflinger, Simpkins, & Combs-Orme, 2000). This might suggest that children's mental health deteriorates in statutory care. However, closer examination indicates that this age effect is largely accounted for by children entering care at older ages with greater mental health difficulties due to their longer pre-care exposure to maltreatment (Hukkanen et al., 1999; Tarren-Sweeney, 2008b).

It is nevertheless possible that children who enter care at an older age, not only do so with poorer pre-existing mental health, but their developmental response to entering care is different to that of children who enter care at a younger age. The therapeutic potential of care may vary according to such factors as children's *age at entry into care*, the extent that their psychological development is compromised at entry into care, and the strength of their existing attachments to their birth families.

What do we know then about the mental health trajectories of children growing up in care? This question can only be answered by longitudinal studies. A recent series of meta-analyses pooled prospective mean score changes in externalizing difficulties (21 studies, combined $N = 1,729$), internalizing difficulties (24 studies, combined $N = 1,984$), and total difficulties (i.e. global mental health; 25 studies, combined $N = 2,523$) from all prospective studies completed to date (Goemans, van Geel, & Vedder, 2015). These meta-analyses showed no mean effect over time. Various moderator analyses failed to show effects when comparing studies on study length, sample size, publication type, attrition, or mean age. Instead, the three meta-analyses identified considerable heterogeneity across the various study findings, with some studies reporting large mean increases in mental health scores over time and others reporting large reductions (Goemans et al., 2015).

Most of the prospective studies published to date followed children over relatively short time periods (most were 6 months to 2 years). These timeframes are too short to predict longer-term mental health trajectories within this population. Only five studies have tracked the mental health of children in care over periods of 5 or more years. The first of these estimated children's mental health over 5 years from social worker reports (Fanshel & Shinn, 1978; Frank, 1980). However, it is doubtful that social workers have sufficient proximal engagement with children in care to be reliable informants of their mental health, and there is no research supporting the validity of this method. A second study compared 5-year changes in the mental health of orphans growing up in foster care versus those placed in children's homes (Bulat, 2010). However, the pre–care development of orphans is not comparable to that of seriously maltreated children. It is important to keep in mind that the effects of growing up in care are not shaped in isolation from the exceptional developmental context of pre–care maltreatment experienced by the vast majority of children placed into care in western, democratic jurisdictions. A third study recruited children shortly after entry into care, but obtained baseline mental health scores from the children's parents rather than their foster parents and then 7- to 8-year follow-up scores from their foster parents, residential carers or parents (depending on whether they remained in foster care, moved to residential care, or returned to their parents' care; Havnen, Breivik, & Jakobsen, 2014). In the absence of inter-rater reliability estimates, the reliability of prospective estimates of the stability of children's mental health over time based on parent- and foster-parent-reported scores at different time points is uncertain. Furthermore, the prospective cohort included children who had left family-based care, such that the findings aren't specific to children growing up in care. The fourth study obtained baseline foster-parent-reported CBCL scores for a large sample (n = 233) of children in care, and 8-year follow-up measures for 111 of the young people (48% retention), by which time many of the participants were adults (Vis, Handegård, Holtan, Fossum, & Thørnblad, 2016). At follow-up, foster-parent-reported CBCL scores were obtained for 38 young people under 18 who were still in care. Instead of reporting prospective mean score changes for these 38 young people, the study reported rates of meaningful change in CBCL total problems scores, as defined by the Reliable Change Index (RCI): 26% (n = 10) showed meaningful improvement, 26% (n = 10) showed meaningful deterioration, and 47% (n = 18) showed no meaningful change. The fifth study was my NSW Children in Care Study, which calculated rates of meaningful change in the mental health of 85 children in foster care over a 7- to 9-year period (Tarren-Sweeney, 2017). The longitudinal analysis is presented in the following section.

Mental health trajectories of children growing up in long-term foster care – results from the Children in Care Study

In the CICS, the mental health of 85 children in foster care was measured using the CBCL and ACC in the baseline survey (1999–2002), and then again in 2009 using the CBCL and ACA, 7–9 years after the baseline survey. Prospective changes in (1) CBCL total problems scale scores and (2) ACC-ACA clinical scores were each (i.e. separately) allocated to four mutually exclusive mental health stability groups:

A   *sustained mental health*
B   *meaningful improvement*
C   *no meaningful change*
D   *meaningful deterioration*

The rates of assignment to the mental health change groups are listed in Table 1.2. On each of the two measures, more than 60% of the children showed either sustained mental health or meaningful improvement in their mental health, while fewer than a quarter showed meaningful deterioration.

While the CBCL total problems score and ACC-ACA shared-item score separately provide an estimation of global mental health for this population, and are strongly correlated (baseline, $r = 0.86$; follow-up, $r = 0.89$), their items nonetheless measure different types and classes of symptoms. Furthermore, these types and classes of symptoms are likely to have different natural histories and change trajectories. Therefore it is useful to examine the

Table 1.2 Rates of assignment to mental health change groups: A. *sustained mental health*; B. *meaningful improvement*; C. *no meaningful change*; D. *meaningful deterioration*

Measure	Group A Sustained mental health[a]		Group B Meaningful improvement[b]		Group C No meaningful change[c]		Group D Meaningful deterioration[d]	
	N	%	N	%	N	%	N	%
CBCL total problems scale	30	35.3%	23	27.1%	11	12.9%	21	24.7%
ACC/ACA shared clinical items	32	37.7%	21	24.7%	16	18.8%	16	18.8%

a Scores within normal range at baseline and follow-up.
b CBCL total score reduction > 11, ACC-ACA shared-item score reduction > 4.
c CBCL total score change < 12, ACC-ACA shared-item score change < 5.
d CBCL total score increase > 11, ACC-ACA shared-item score increase > 4.

concordance of assignment to change groups by each measure. Table 1.3 lists a 4 × 4 matrix showing numbers of young people assigned to each combination of the four groups for the two measures. This table reveals a fairly high degree of concordance on change group assignment for the two measures. Importantly, no young person showed meaningful improvement on one measure and meaningful deterioration on the other. In summary, the findings indicate that 31.8% of young people ($n = 27$) manifested *sustained mental health* on both measures; 32.9% ($n = 28$) manifested *meaningful improvement* in their mental health on one or both measures; 29.4% ($n = 25$) manifested *meaningful deterioration* in their mental health on one or both measures; and the remaining 5.9% ($n = 5$) showed no meaningful change on either measure.

The rates of meaningful change identified in the CICS suggest that substantial proportions of children in foster care experience very different mental health trajectories. This is not surprising, given that the experience of growing up in care is heterogeneous,

Table 1.3 Matrix of participants' ($N = 85$) assignment to mental health change groups, based on CBCL versus ACC-ACA score changes

		Group Assignment based on ACC-ACA score changes			
		A: *Sustained mental health*	**B**: *Meaningful improvement*	**C**: *No meaningful change*	**D**: *Meaningful deterioration*
Group assignment based on CBCL score changes	**A**: Sustained mental health	27	3	0	0
	B: Meaningful improvement	3	16	4	0
	C: No meaningful change	0	2	5	4
	D: Meaningful deterioration	2	0	7	12

and that children enter care with heterogeneous developmental context (such as varying ages at entry into care). It is very likely that for some children, long-term care provides the opportunity to grow up feeling loved, nurtured, and secure, translating into relational permanence. For these children, alternate care provides the conditions for developmental recovery, whereby therapeutic effects accumulate and consolidate over time. For other children, long-term care may compromise their development and well-being.

This raises a question, then, about how we should define and measure 'successful' outcomes for children whose early development is seriously compromised by severe and chronic maltreatment. Children who continue to manifest clinical-level mental health difficulties through their time in care may nonetheless have benefitted from being in care, relative to what would have unfolded had they remained in the care of their maltreating families. In other words, success might be defined as experiencing less adverse developmental outcomes than otherwise would have been the case. Unfortunately, we presently lack good comparative data on the developmental trajectories of severely and chronically maltreated children who are raised by their parents versus those raised by foster parents and kin (Goemans, van Geel, van Beem, & Vedder, 2016).

Rather than asking whether long-term care is generally therapeutic or harmful for the development of previously maltreated children, future investigations should focus on the questions "what are the systemic and interpersonal characteristics of care that promote and sustain children's psychological development throughout childhood, and what characteristics are developmentally harmful?" and "for which children is care therapeutic, and for which children is it not?" These questions are critical for both social care policy and practice and for the design of clinical interventions. Various developmental theories (including attachment theory and social learning theory), as well as research into the neurodevelopmental effects of early maltreatment, would predict that the therapeutic and harm potentials of long-term care will be moderated by such factors as children's age when entering care, their caregivers' commitment and bonding to them, and the stability of their placements. There are likely to be complex transactional mechanisms that dictate children's developmental trajectories as they grow up in care. Unfortunately, there has been very little substantive research on this question to date. It is also important to keep in mind that developmental change within care is moderated by this population's earlier exposure to severe social adversity. A recent study found that the developmental effects of more than 6 months' exposure in early childhood to profound psychosocial deprivation (institutional care) persist for many through childhood and adolescence, despite being subsequently raised by loving adoptive families (Sonuga-Barke et al., 2017). These persistent effects include symptoms of autism spectrum disorder, disinhibited social engagement, and inattention and over-activity. This supports the notion that recovery from some forms of psychopathology caused by early severe adversity tends to follow a long developmental trajectory even where a child's developmental conditions have markedly improved.

References

Achenbach, T. (1991). *Manual for the Child Behavior Checklist/4–18, and 1991 profile*. Burlington: University of Vermont.

Achenbach, T., & Rescorla, L. (2001). *Manual for ASEBA school-age forms and profiles*. Burlington: University of Vermont, Research Center for Children, Youth, & Families.

Adams, J., & McClellan, J. (1995). Sexually inappropriate behaviors in seriously mentally ill children and adolescents. *Child Abuse & Neglect, 19*(5), 555–568.

American Psychiatric Association. (2000). *Diagnostic and statistical manual of mental disorders: Text revision* (4th ed.). Washington, DC: American Psychiatric Association.

Armsden, G., Pecora, P., Payne, V., & Szatkiewicz, J. (2000). Children placed in long-term foster care: An intake profile using the Child Behavior Checklist/4–18. *Journal of Emotional & Behavioral Disorders, 8*(1), 49–64.

Becker, J. (1998). What we know about the characteristics and treatment of adolescents who have committed sexual offences. *Child Maltreatment, 3*, 317–329.

Bender, I., & Yarnell, H. (1941). An observation nursery: A study of 250 children on the psychiatric division of Bellevue hospital. *American Journal of Psychiatry, 97*, 1158–1174.

Benoit, J., & Kennedy, W. (1992). The abuse history of male adolescent sex offenders. *Journal of Interpersonal Violence, 7*, 543–548.

Biehal, N., Ellison, S., Baker, C., & Sinclair, I. (2009). *Characteristics, outcomes and meanings of three types of permanent placement: Adoption by strangers, adoption by carers, and long-term foster care.* London: Department for Children Schools and Families (DCSF).

Biehal, N., Ellison, S., Baker, C., & Sinclair, I. (2010). *Belonging and permanence: Outcomes in long-term foster care and adoption.* London: BAAF.

Blower, A., Addo, A., Hodgson, J., Lamington, L., & Towlson, K. (2004). Mental health of 'looked after' children: A needs assessment. *Clinical Child Psychology and Psychiatry, 9,* 117–129.

Bonner, B., & Walker, C. (1999). Children with sexual behavior problems: Assessment and treatment. In Final report, Grant No. 90-CA-1469, National Center on Child Abuse and Neglect, Administration for Children, Youth, and Families, U.S. Department of Human Services.

Bowlby, J. (1988). *A secure base: Clinical applications of attachment theory.* London: Routledge.

Bronsard, G., Lançon, C., Loundou, A., Auquier, P., Rufo, M., & Siméoni, M. (2011). Prevalence rate of DSM mental disorders among adolescents living in residential group homes of the French child welfare system. *Children and Youth Services Review, 33,* 1886–1890.

Bulat, L. (2010). A longitudinal study of depressiveness in children in public care. *International Journal of Social Welfare, 19,* 412–423.

Burton, D. (2000). Were adolescent sexual offenders children with sexual behavior problems? *Sexual Abuse, 12*(1), 37–48.

Chaffin, M., Berliner, L., Block, R., Johnson, T. C., Friedrich, W., Louis, D., . . . Madden, C. (2008). Report of the ATSA Task Force on children with sexual behavior problems. *Child Maltreatment, 13,* 199–218.

Cheng, S., Foster, R., & Hester, N. (2003). A review of factors predicting children's pain experiences. *Issues in Comprehensive Pediatric Nursing, 26,* 203–216.

Cicchetti, D., Toth, S., & Maughan, A. (2000). An ecological-transactional model of child maltreatment. In A. Sameroff & M. Lewis (Eds.), *Handbook of developmental psychopathology* (2nd ed., pp. 689–722). Dordrecht, Netherlands: Kluwer Academic.

Cosentino, C., Meyer-Bahlburg, H., Alpert, J., Weinberg, S., & Gaines, R. (1995). Sexual behavior problems and psychopathology symptoms in sexually abused girls. *Journal of the American Academy of Child & Adolescent Psychiatry, 34*(8), 1033–1042.

Crawford, M. (2006). Health of children in out-of-home care: Can we do better? *Journal of Paediatrics & Child Health, 42,* 77–78.

Crittenden, P. (2006). A dynamic-maturational model of attachment. *Australian and New Zealand Journal of Family Therapy, 27*(2), 105–115.

D'Andrea, W., Ford, J., Stolbach, B., Spinazzola, J., & van der Kolk, B. (2012). Understanding interpersonal trauma in children: Why we need a developmentally appropriate trauma diagnosis. *American Journal of Orthopsychiatry, 82*(2), 187–200.

DeJong, M. (2010). Some reflections on the use of psychiatric diagnosis in the looked after or 'in care' child population. *Clinical Child Psychology and Psychiatry, 15*(4), 589–599.

DeJong, M., Hodges, J., & Malik, O. (2016). Children after adoption: Exploring their psychological needs. *Clinical Child Psychology & Psychiatry, 21*(4), 536–550.

de Kerdanet, M., Seveno, T., & Lecornu, M. (1993). Growth retardation of psychosocial origin: Clinical and biological aspects in four cases. *Pediatrie, 48*(11), 783–787.

Delfabbro, P. (2016). *A profile of foster care and kinship care in NSW.* Paper presented at the Association of Child Welfare Agencies Conference, Sydney. Retrieved from www.community.nsw.gov.au/__data/assets/file/0006/388437/ACWA_slides_Paul_POCLS.pdf

Delfabbro, P., & Barber, J. (2003). Before it's too late: Enhancing the early detection and prevention of long-term placement disruption. *Children Australia, 28*(2), 14–18.

Demyttenaere, S., Finley, G., Johnston, C., & McGrath, P. (2001). Pain treatment thresholds in children after major surgery. *Clinical Journal of Pain, 17*(2), 173–177.

Dozier, M., Bick, J., & Bernard, K. (2011). Attachment-based treatment for young, vulnerable children. In J. Osofsky & A. Lieberman (Eds.), *Clinical work with traumatized young children.* New York, NY: Guilford Press.

Dozier, M., Stovall, K. C., Albus, K. E., & Bates, B. (2001). Attachment for infants in foster care: The role of caregiver state of mind. *Child Development, 72*(5), 1467–1477.

Drach, K., Wientzen, J., & Ricci, L. (2001). The diagnostic utility of sexual behavior problems in diagnosing sexual abuse in a forensic child abuse evaluation clinic. *Child Abuse & Neglect, 25*, 489–503.

Dubner, A. E., & Motta, R. W. (1999). Sexually and physically abused foster care children and posttraumatic stress disorder. *Journal of Consulting and Clinical Psychology, 67*(3), 367–373.

Dubowitz, H., Zuravin, S., Starr, R. H., Feigelman, S., & Harrington, D. (1993). Behavior problems of children in kinship care. *Journal of Developmental and Behavioral Pediatrics, 14*(6), 386–393.

Elander, J., & Rutter, M. (1996). Use and development of the Rutter parents' and teachers' scales. *International Journal of Methods in Psychiatric Research, 6*(2), 63–78.

Famularo, R., & Augustyn, M. (1996). Persistence of pediatric post traumatic stress disorder after 2 years. *Child Abuse and Neglect, 20*(12), 1245–1248.

Fanshel, D., & Shinn, E. (1978). *Children in foster care: A longitudinal investigation.* New York, NY: Columbia University Press.

Fehrenbach, P., Smith, W., Montastersky, C., & Deisher, R. (1986). Adolescent sexual offenders: Offender and offense characteristics. *American Journal of Orthopsychiatry, 56*, 225–233.

Fein, E., & Maluccio, A. (1992). Permanency planning: Another remedy in jeopardy? *Social Services Review, 66*(3), 335–348.

Fergusson, D., & Lynskey, M. (1996). Adolescent resiliency to family adversity. *Journal of Child Psychology & Psychiatry, 33*, 1059–1075.

Fonagy, P. (2003). The development of psychopathology from infancy to adulthood: The mysterious unfolding of disturbance in time. *Infant Mental Health Journal, 24*(3), 212–239.

Frank, G. (1980). Treatment needs of children in foster care. *American Journal of Orthopsychiatry, 50*(2), 256–263.

Friedrich, W. (1997). *Child Sexual Behavior Inventory: Professional manual.* Odessa, FL: Psychological Assessment Resources.

Friedrich, W. (2005). Correlates of sexual behavior in young children. *Journal of Child Custody, 2*(3), 41–55.

Friedrich, W. (2007). *Children with sexual behavior problems: Family-based, attachment-focused therapy.* New York, NY: Norton.

Friedrich, W., Davies, W., Feher, E., & Wright, J. (2003). Sexual behavior problems in preteen children: Developmental, ecological and behavioral correlates. *Annals of the New York Academy of Sciences, 989*, 95–104.

Friedrich, W., Fisher, J., Broughton, D., Houston, M., & Shafran, C. (1998). Normative sexual behavior in children: A contemporary sample. *Pediatrics, 101*(4), E91–E98.

Friedrich, W., Fisher, J., Dittner, C., Acton, R., Berliner, L., Butler, J., . . . Wright, J. (2001). Child sexual behaviour inventory: Normative, psychiatric, and sexual abuse comparisons. *Child Maltreatment, 6*(1), 37–49.

Friedrich, W., & Grambsch, P. (1992). Child Sexual behavior inventory: Normative and clinical comparisons. *Psychological Assessment, 4*(3), 303–311.

Friedrich, W., Trane, S., & Gully, K. (2005). Re: It is a mistake to conclude that sexual abuse and sexualized behavior are not related: A reply to Drach, Wientzen, and Ricci (2001). *Child Abuse & Neglect, 29*, 297–302.

Goemans, A., van Geel, M., van Beem, M., & Vedder, P. (2016). Developmental outcomes of foster children: A meta-analytic comparison with children from the general population and children at risk who remained at home. *Child Maltreatment, 21*(3), 198–217.

Goemans, A., van Geel, M., & Vedder, P. (2015). Over three decades of longitudinal research on the development of foster children: A meta-analysis. *Child Abuse and Neglect, 42*, 121–134.

Goldfarb, W. (1949). Rorschach test differences between family-reared, institution-reared, and schizophrenic children. *American Journal of Orthopsychiatry, 1*, 624–633.

Goodman, R. (2001). Psychometric properties of the Strengths and Difficulties Questionnaire. *Journal of the American Academy of Child & Adolescent Psychiatry, 40*, 1337–1345.

Gray, A., Pithers, W., Busconi, A., & Houchens, P. (1999). Developmental and etiological characteristics of children with sexual behavior problems: Treatment implications. *Child Abuse & Neglect, 23*(6), 601–621.

Green, W., Campbell, M., & David, R. (1984). Psychosocial dwarfism: A critical review of the evidence. *Journal of the American Academy of Child & Adolescent Psychiatry, 23*(1), 39–48.

Grilo, C., & Masheb, R. (2001). Childhood psychological, physical, and sexual maltreatment in outpatients with binge eating disorder: Frequency and associations with gender, obesity and eating-related psychopathology. *Obesity Research, 9*(5), 320–325.

Halfon, N., Mendonca, A., & Berkowitz, G. (1995). Health status of children in foster care: The experience of the Center for the Vulnerable Child. *Archives of Pediatrics & Adolescent Medicine, 149*(4), 386–392.

Havnen, K., Breivik, K., & Jakobsen, R. (2014). Stability and change: A 7- to 8-year follow-up study of mental health problems in Norwegian children in long-term out-of-home care. *Child & Family Social Work, 19*, 292–303.

Heflinger, C., Simpkins, C., & Combs-Orme, T. (2000). Using the CBCL to determine the clinical status of children in state custody. *Children & Youth Services Review, 22*(1), 55–73.

Hermann, C., Hohmeister, J., Demirakca, S., Zohsel, K., & Flor, H. (2006). Long-term alteration of pain sensitivity in school-aged children with early pain experiences. *Pain, 125*, 278–285.

Holtan, A., Ronning, J., Handegård, B., & Sourander, A. (2005). A comparison of mental health problems in kinship and nonkinship foster care. *European Child and Adolescent Psychiatry, 14*(4), 200–207.

Howe, D. (2003). Attachment disorders: Disinhibited attachment behaviours and secure base distortions with special reference to adopted children. *Attachment and Human Development, 5*(3), 265–270.

Howe, D., & Fearnley, S. (2003). Disorders of attachment in adopted and fostered children: Recognition and treatment. *Clinical Child Psychology & Psychiatry, 8*, 369–387.

Hukkanen, R., Sourander, A., Bergroth, L., & Piha, J. (1999). Psychosocial factors and adequacy of services for children in children's homes. *European Child and Adolescent Psychiatry, 8*, 268–275.

Johnson, T. C. (1993). Assessment of sexual behavior problems in pre-school and latency-aged children. *Child and Adolescent Psychiatric Clinics of North America, 2*(3), 431–450.

Kahn, T., & Lafond, M. (1988). Treatment of the adolescent sexual offender. *Child & Adolescent Social Work Journal, 5*, 135–148.

Kendall-Tackett, K., Williams, L., & Finkelhor, D. (1993). Impact of sexual abuse on children: A review and synthesis of recent empirical studies. *Psychological Bulletin, 113*(1), 164–180.

Kent, A., Waller, G., & Dagnan, D. (1999). A greater role of emotional than physical or sexual abuse in predicting disordered eating attitudes: The role of mediating variables. *International Journal of Eating Disorders, 25*, 159–167.

Klee, L., Kronstadt, D., & Zlotnick, C. (1997). Foster care's youngest: A preliminary report. *American Journal of Orthopsychiatry, 67*(2), 290–299.

Kreppner, J., O'Connor, T., Rutter, M., Beckett, C., Castle, J., Croft, C., . . . Groothues, C. (2001). Can inattention/overactivity be an institutional deprivation syndrome? *Journal of Abnormal Child Psychology, 29*(6), 513–528.

Lehmann, S., Havik, O., Havik, T., & Heiervang, E. (2013). Mental disorders in foster children: A study of prevalence, comorbidity and risk factors. *Child and Adolescent Psychiatry and Mental Health, 7*(39), 1–12.

Letourneau, E., Schoenwald, S., & Sheidow, A. (2004). Children and adolescents with sexual behavior problems. *Child Maltreatment, 9*(1), 49–61.

Levy, D. (1937). Primary affect hunger. *American Journal of Psychiatry, 94*, 643–652.

Lieberman, A., & Zeanah, C. (1995). Disorders of attachment in infancy. *Child & Adolescent Psychiatric Clinics of North America, 4*(3), 571–587.

Lutman, E., & Farmer, E. (2013). What contributes to outcomes for neglected children who are reunified with their parents? Findings from a five-year follow-up study. *British Journal of Social Work, 43*, 559–578.

McCann, J., Wilson, S., & Dunn, G. (1996). Prevalence of psychiatric disorders in young people in the care system. *British Medical Journal, 313*, 1529–1530.

McClellan, J., McCurry, C., Ronnei, M., Adams, J., Storck, M., Eisner, E., & Smith, C. (1997). Relationship between sexual abuse, gender, and sexually inappropriate behaviors in seriously mentally ill youths. *Journal of the American Academy of Child & Adolescent Psychiatry, 36*(7), 959–965.

McMillen, J., Zima, B., Scott, L., Auslander, W., Munson, M., Ollie, M., & Spitznagel, E. (2005). Prevalence of psychiatric disorders among older youths in the foster care system. *Journal of the American Academy of Child & Adolescent Psychiatry, 44*(1), 88–95.

Meakings, S., & Selwyn, J. (2016). 'She was a foster mother who said she didn't give cuddles': The adverse early foster care experiences of children who later struggle with adoptive family life. *Clinical Child Psychology & Psychiatry, 21*(4), 509–519.

Meltzer, H., Corbin, T., Gatward, R., Goodman, R., & Ford, T. (2003). *The mental health of young people looked after by local authorities in England.* London: Office for National Statistics, The Stationery Office.

Melzack, R. (1999). From the gate to the neuromatrix. *Pain*, (Suppl. 6), S121–S126.

Mian, M., Marton, P., & LeBaron, D. (1996). The effects of sexual abuse on 3- to 5-year-old girls. *Child Abuse & Neglect*, *20*(8), 731–745.

Milan, S., & Pinderhughes, E. (2000). Factors influencing maltreated children's early adjustment in foster care. *Development and Psychopathology*, *12*(1), 63–81.

Minnis, H., Everett, K., Pelosi, A., Dunn, J., & Knapp, M. (2006). Children in foster care: Mental health, service use and costs. *European Child and Adolescent Psychiatry*, *15*, 63–70.

Minnis, H., & Keck, G. (2003). A clinical/research dialogue on reactive attachment disorder. *Attachment and Human Development*, *5*(3), 297–301.

Molinari, E. (2001). Eating disorders and sexual abuse. *Eating and Weight Disorders*, *6*(2), 68–80.

Newton, R., Litrownik, A., & Landsverk, J. (2000). Children and youth in foster care: Disentangling the relationship between problem behaviors and number of placements. *Child Abuse and Neglect*, *24*(10), 1363–1374.

Nutt, L. (2006). *The lives of foster carers: Private sacrifices, public restrictions*. Abingdon, Oxon: Routledge.

O'Connor, T., Bredenkamp, D., Rutter, M., & the English and Romanian Adoptees Study Team. (1999). Attachment disturbances and disorders in children exposed to early severe deprivation. *Infant Mental Health Journal*, *20*(1), 10–29.

O'Connor, T., & Rutter, M. (2000). Attachment disorder behavior following early severe deprivation: Extension and longitudinal follow-up. *Journal of the American Academy of Child & Adolescent Psychiatry*, *39*(6), 703–712.

Oliván, G. (2003). Catch-up growth assessment in long-term physically neglected and emotionally abused preschool age male children. *Child Abuse & Neglect*, *27*(1), 103–108.

Oswald, S., Heil, K., & Goldbeck, L. (2010). History of maltreatment and mental health problems in foster children: A review of the literature. *Journal of Pediatric Psychology*, *35*(5), 462–472.

Paolucci, E., Genuis, M., & Violato, C. (2001). A meta-analysis of the published research on the effects of child sexual abuse. *Journal of Psychology*, *135*(1), 17–36.

Pecora, P., White, C., Jackson, L., & Wiggins, T. (2009). Mental health of current and former recipients of foster care: A review of recent studies in the USA. *Child & Family Social Work*, *14*, 132–146.

Powell, G., Brasel, J., & Blizzard, R. (1967). Emotional deprivation and growth retardation simulating idiopathic hypopituitarism: I. Clinical evaluation of the syndrome. *New England Journal of Medicine*, *276*, 1271–1278.

Putnam, F. (2003). Ten-year research update review: Child sexual abuse. *Journal of the American Academy of Child & Adolescent Psychiatry*, *42*(3), 269–278.

Ricci, L., Drach, K., & Wientzen, J. (2005). Further comment on the lack of utility of sexual behavior problems as measured by the Child Sexual Behavior Inventory in diagnosing sexual abuse: A reply to Friedrich, Gully, and Trane (2004). *Child Abuse & Neglect, 29*, 303–306.

Richters, M., & Volkmar, F. (1994). Reactive attachment disorder of infancy or early childhood. *Journal of the American Academy of Child & Adolescent Psychiatry, 33*(3), 328–332.

Rowe, J., & Lambert, L. (1973). *Children who wait.* London: Association of British Fostering Agencies.

Rutter, M. (1999). Psychosocial adversity and child psychopathology. *British Journal of Psychiatry, 174*, 480–493.

Rutter, M. (2000). Children in substitute care: Some conceptual considerations and research implications. *Children & Youth Services Review, 22*(9–10), 685–703.

Schofield, G. (2002). The significance of a secure base: A psychosocial model of long-term foster care. *Child & Family Social Work, 7*, 259–272.

Selwyn, J., Wijedasa, D., & Meakings, S. (2014). *Beyond the Adoption Order: Challenges, interventions and adoption disruption.* London: Department for Education. Retrieved from www.gov.uk/government/publications/beyond-the-adoption-order-challenges-intervention-disruption

Silovsky, J., & Niec, L. (2002). Characteristics of young children with sexual behavior problems: A pilot study. *Child Maltreatment, 7*(3), 187–197.

Skuse, D., Albanese, A., Stanhope, R., Gilmour, J., & Voss, L. (1996). A new stress-related syndrome of growth failure and hyperphagia in children, associated with reversibility of growth-hormone insufficiency. *Lancet, 348*, 353–358.

Smyke, A., Dumitrescu, A., & Zeanah, C. H. (2002). Attachment disturbances in young children: I. The continuum of caretaking. *Journal of the American Academy of Child & Adolescent Psychiatry, 41*(8), 972–982.

Sonuga-Barke, E., Kennedy, M., Kumsta, R., Knights, N., Golm, D., Rutter, M., . . . Kreppner, J. (2017). Child-to-adult neurodevelopmental and mental health trajectories after early life deprivation: The young adult follow-up of the longitudinal English and Romanian Adoptees Study. *Lancet, 389*, 1539–1548. https://doi.org/10.1016/S0140-6736(17)30045-4

Stein, E., Rae-Grant, N., Ackland, S., & Avison, W. (1994). Psychiatric disorders of children 'in care': Methodology and demographic correlates. *Canadian Journal of Psychiatry: Revue Canadienne de Psychiatrie, 39*(6), 341–347.

Stiegler, L. (2005). Understanding pica behavior: A review for clinical and education professionals. *Focus on Autism and Other Developmental Disabilities, 20*(1), 27–23.

Taitz, L., & King, J. (1988). Growth patterns in child abuse. *Acta Paediatrica Scandinavica, 343*(Suppl.), 62–72.

Tarren-Sweeney, M. (2006). Patterns of aberrant eating among pre-adolescent children in foster care. *Journal of Abnormal Child Psychology, 34,* 623–634.

Tarren-Sweeney, M. (2007). The Assessment Checklist for Children (ACC): A behavioral rating scale for children in foster, kinship and residential care. *Children & Youth Services Review, 29,* 672–691.

Tarren-Sweeney, M. (2008a). The mental health of children in out-of-home care. *Current Opinion in Psychiatry, 21,* 345–349.

Tarren-Sweeney, M. (2008b). Retrospective and concurrent predictors of the mental health of children in care. *Children & Youth Services Review, 30,* 1–25.

Tarren-Sweeney, M. (2013). The Assessment Checklist for Adolescents (ACA): A scale for measuring the mental health of young people in foster, kinship, residential and adoptive care. *Children and Youth Services Review, 35,* 384–393.

Tarren-Sweeney, M. (2017). Rates of meaningful change in the mental health of children in long-term out-of-home care: A seven- to nine-year prospective study. *Child Abuse and Neglect, 72,* 1–9.

Tarren-Sweeney, M., & Hazell, P. (2006). The mental health of children in foster and kinship care in New South Wales, Australia. *Journal of Paediatrics & Child Health, 42,* 91–99.

United Nations General Assembly. (2010). *Guidelines for the alternative care of children* (Vol. 64th Session (64/142)). New York, NY: United Nations.

van der Kolk, B. (2005). Developmental trauma disorder. *Psychiatric Annals, 35*(5), 401–408.

van IJzendoorn, M., & Bakermans-Kranenburg, M. (2003). Attachment disorders and disorganized attachment: Similar and different. *Attachment and Human Development, 5*(3), 313–320.

Vanschoonlandt, F., Vanderfaeillie, J., Van Holen, F., De Maeyer, S., & Andries, C. (2012). Kinship and non-kinship foster care: Differences in contact with parents and foster child's mental health problems. *Children and Youth Services Review, 34,* 1533–1539.

Vis, S., Handegård, B., Holtan, A., Fossum, S., & Thørnblad, R. (2016). Social functioning and mental health among children who have been living in kinship and non-kinship foster care: Results from an 8-year follow-up with a Norwegian sample. *Child & Family Social Work, 21,* 557–567.

Wade, J., Biehal, N., Farrelly, N., & Sinclair, I. (2010). *Maltreated children in the looked after system: A comparison of outcomes for those who go home and those who do not.* London: Department for Education. Retrieved from www.gov.uk/government/publications/maltreated-children-in-the-looked-after-system-a-comparison-of-outcomes-for-those-who-go-home-and-those-who-do-not

White, S., Halpin, B., Strom, G., & Santilli, G. (1988). Behavioral comparisons of young sexually abused, neglected, and non-referred children. *Journal of Clinical Child Psychology, 17,* 53–61.

Wolkind, S., & Rushton, A. (1994). Residential and family foster care. In M. Rutter, E. A. Taylor, & L. A. Hersov (Eds.), *Child and adolescent psychiatry: Modern approaches* (3rd ed.). Oxford: Blackwell Scientific.

Woolf, C., & Salter, M. (2000). Neuronal plasticity: Increasing the gain in pain. *Science, 288,* 1765–1769.

World Health Organization. (2002). *The world health report: 2002.* Geneva: World Health Organization.

Wyatt, D., Simms, M., & Horwitz, S. (1997). Widespread growth retardation and variable growth recovery in foster children in the first year after initial placement. *Archives of Pediatrics & Adolescent Medicine, 151*(8), 813–816.

Zero to Three. (2005). *Diagnostic classification of mental health and developmental disorders of infancy and early childhood: Revised edition (DC: 0–3R).* Washington, DC: Zero to Three Press.

2 Clinical interventions and support services for children in alternative care (and their carers)

Access to mental health interventions and support for children in alternative care

Chapter 1 of this book summarizes the evidence that more than half of children in alternative care (regardless of where they reside in the western world) have mental health problems of sufficient scale and severity to warrant the provision of mental health services. Arguably, no other child population in our present society has greater need for mental health services.

In spite of this apparent need, sizeable proportions of children and young people in care who might benefit from intervention do not receive adequate clinical assessment or access to mental health services. This is despite governments holding parental responsibility obligations for these children. This occurs because of one or more of the following:

1   Their difficulties remain undetected
2   Services are not sought by their social workers or caregivers
3   Their social workers or caregivers aren't able to access available services
4   There is a lack of suitable services.

Mental health service use in the Children in Care Study

The baseline survey of the Children in Care Study (described in Chapter 1) included several questions on children's and their foster parents' use of mental health services. Their access to child-directed individual therapies, and to caregiver interventions and clinical guidance, are summarized in Table 2.1. Close to half of the children (44%) were reported to have obtained individual therapy in the 2 years prior to the survey, with rates of service use being similar for boys and girls. In the same timeframe, 72% of children who were said to have a diagnosed mental disorder received individual therapy. Recipients of individual therapy on average attended 1.7 therapy services (152 children/248 service events), which were mostly provided by

Table 2.1 Pattern of mental health service utilization within present placements

A: Individual child psychotherapy/counselling (in last 2 years)					
	N	% of treated children (n = 152)	% of total sample (n = 343)	N service events[a]	% of service events (n = 248)
Number of individual services					
1	88	57.9	25.7	88	35.5
2	37	24.3	10.8	74	29.8
3	10	6.6	2.9	30	12.1
4	7	4.6	2.0	28	11.3
5–7	5	3.3	1.5	28	11.3
Not stated	5	3.3	1.5	n.a.	n.a.
Provider of individual service					
Psychologist	91	59.9	26.5		36.7
School counsellor	42	27.6	12.2		16.9
Paediatrician	29	19.1	8.5		11.7
Psychiatrist	23	15.1	6.7		9.3
Social worker	21	13.8	6.1		8.5
Generic counsellor	13	8.6	3.8		5.2
Welfare worker	11	7.2	3.2		4.4
Maltreatment counsellor[b]	9	5.9	2.6		3.6
Other counsellor[c]	9	5.9	2.6		3.6
Not stated	5	3.3	1.5		n.a.

(*Continued*)

Table 2.1 (Continued)

B. *Caregiver clinical guidance/parenting advice/behaviour management*

	N	% of managed children (n = 158)	% of total sample (n = 347)	N advice events[d]	% of advice events (n = 233)
Number of advisors					
1	86	54.4	24.8	86	36.9
2	40	25.3	11.5	80	34.3
3	16	10.1	4.6	48	20.6
4–6	4	2.5	1.2	19	8.2
Not stated	12	7.6	3.5	n.a.	n.a.
Provider of advice					
Psychologist	81	51.3	23.3		34.8
School counsellor	20	12.7	5.8		8.6
Paediatrician	18	11.4	5.2		7.7
Psychiatrist	16	10.1	4.6		6.9
Generic counsellor	14	8.9	4.0		6.0
Social worker	13	8.2	3.8		5.6
Other school	12	7.6	3.5		5.2
Maltreatment counsellor[b]	10	6.3	2.9		4.3
General practitioner	9	5.7	2.6		3.9
Welfare worker	7	4.4	2.0		3.0
Training course	6	3.8	1.7		2.6
Other[e]	27	17.1	7.8		11.6
Not stated	12	7.6	3.5		n.a.

a Number of service events equals the number of treated children times the number of services each child receives (total events = 248).

b Specialist counselling for maltreated children (PANOC = 5; sexual assault counselling = 4).

c Other counsellors: family therapist (*n* = 3); mental health nurse (*n* = 2); other nurse (*n* = 2); special education teacher (*n* = 1).

d Number of advice events equals the number of children requiring management times the number of sources of advice each carer receives (total events = 233).

e Other sources of advice: health services (4); caseworkers (4); naturopath (3); family therapist (3); speech pathologist (3); mental health nurse (2); clergy (1); other carers (1); neurologist (1); behavioural therapist (1); occupational therapist (1); neuro-psychologist (1); health worker (1); support worker (1).

psychologists and school counsellors (who in NSW are also registered psychologists).

A similar proportion of foster parents (45%) said they had received clinical guidance for managing their child's behaviour or feelings. Their receipt of clinical guidance was not related to their foster child's gender. Foster parents were twice as likely to have received clinical guidance if they also reported that their child had a diagnosed mental disorder. While they obtained such guidance from a wide range of professions, services, training courses and other foster parents, psychologists were the primary source of guidance. There was also considerable overlap in psychologists' provision of therapy to children and clinical guidance to caregivers. Other service providers (such as paediatricians, social workers, psychiatrists, and school counsellors) were much more involved in providing direct services to children than guidance to caregivers.

Thirty-one percent of foster children received treatment by way of both individual therapy and caregiver clinical guidance. These are henceforth referred to as *double service* children. Another 28% of children either received individual therapy or caregiver clinical support. These are referred to as *single service* children. Of the remaining 41% (141/343) of children who received neither form of service, 114 of their foster parents had not sought either type of service, while 27 foster parents had unsuccessfully sought one or both types of service. Therefore, the proportion of children for whom any service was sought but not obtained was just 12% (27/229). Among single service children, caregiver clinical guidance had been sought for 21 of the 45 children receiving therapy, and child individual therapy had been sought for 8 of the 50 children whose caregivers received clinical guidance.

The caregiver-reported rate of prescription of psychiatric medication among subject children was 16% (55/347). The most commonly prescribed psychiatric medications were stimulants ($n = 49$) and clonidine ($n = 16$). The former are typically prescribed for treatment of ADHD and the latter for treatment of comorbid aggression (Hazell & Stuart, 2003). Clonidine was prescribed in conjunction with stimulants for 13 children, and as sole medication for three. Eighty-five percent (47/55) of the children prescribed psychiatric medication were reported to have received other mental health services (child therapy and/or caregiver clinical guidance).

Caregivers had unsuccessfully sought other services for five of the remaining eight children.

International research on rates of access to clinical services

While it is reported that maltreated U.S. children are more likely to access public mental health services following entry into care than when they were in their parents' care (Leslie et al., 2005), rates of service use fall well short of the estimated rate requiring mental health services. Among a nationally representative sample of U.S. children in foster care (a sub-sample of the National Survey of Child and Adolescent Well-Being [NSCAW]), only one third to one half of children with clinical-level mental health difficulties received a mental health service in the preceding 12 months (National Survey of Child and Adolescent Well-Being, 2003). Similarly, whereas 61% of a survey sample of children and adolescents in foster care (N = 326) in South Australia had clinical-level difficulties (as estimated from foster-parent-report CBCL scores), and 53% were identified by their foster parents as being in need of clinical services, only 27% managed to obtain a service in the preceding 6 months (Sawyer, Carbone, Searle, & Robinson, 2007). A mental health survey of 182 Scottish children in foster care found that their overall mental health difficulties predicted ongoing involvement with social workers, and that those with elevated hyperactivity scores were more likely to receive community paediatric services (Minnis, Everett, Pelosi, Dunn, & Knapp, 2006). While this study found that children with the greatest mental health difficulties received a high level of support from various social and health services, they had very poor access to CAMHS. Indeed, their access to CAMHS was unrelated to the number and severity of their mental health symptoms.

By contrast, a relatively low level of unmet demand for mental health services was identified in the CICS survey: only 12% of caregivers were unsuccessful in obtaining a clinical service. This unexpected finding can be partially explained by the presence of a psychology service within the state child welfare department in NSW, Australia. Psychologists play a central role in mental health and developmental service provision for NSW children in care because the child welfare department maintains a specialist psychological service to work with these children. This does not preclude such children's access to the health department's CAMHS and paediatric services, or to behavioural-developmental services within education. Another feature of the NSW jurisdiction that is likely to facilitate children's access to services is a 'best endeavours' provision, inserted in child welfare legislation a few years before the present survey was conducted. The provision enables children's caseworkers to submit 'best endeavours' requests to other government agencies to provide services that "promote and safeguard the safety, welfare and well-being of a child or young person" (Children and Young Persons [Care and Protection] Act [NSW], 1998). Agencies in turn are legally required to make 'best endeavours' to respond to such referrals. School counsellors were the next most prominent providers of both types of services, although their role description perhaps limits their involvement with caregivers. In NSW, school counsellors are registered (i.e. 'chartered' or 'licensed') psychologists. There has been universal provision of school counselling services in NSW state schools for many decades, and parents and caregivers often look to them as primary care mental health providers. The situation in NSW then is probably more favourable than in most other jurisdictions in the western world. Despite this, caregivers neither accessed nor sought mental health services for around a quarter of children with clinically significant mental health difficulties, reinforcing previous findings that foster caregivers represent a critical gateway to mental health services.

Among children and young people adopted from care, there is evidence that (in the United Kingdom at least) their access to mental health services increases after they are adopted. In one study of children adopted from care, access to CAMHS increased from 26% prior to adoption (i.e. while they were in foster care) to more than 55% following adoption (Sturgess & Selwyn, 2007). This exceeds even the high rate of mental health service among the NSW foster care sample (Tarren-Sweeney, 2010).

Relationships between children's mental health and access to services

Several U.S. studies have found moderate correlations between children's symptom scores on standardized checklists and their use of mental health services (Bellamy, 2007; Burns et al., 2004; Garland, Landsverk, Hough, & Ellis-Macleod, 1996; Leslie et al., 2000; Zima, Bussing, Yang, & Belin, 2000). This suggests there is some relationship between children's level of need for therapy services and their receipt of such services.

The CICS baseline survey also found a clear relationship between the scale of children's mental health difficulties and their access to clinical services. There were meaningful differences (in terms of both effect size and likely impairment) in the distributions of global mental health estimates for *double service, single service*, and *nil service* children. The average CBCL total problems score for these three groups were 62, 53, and 33, respectively; their average ACC total clinical scores were 39, 35, and 19, respectively. Despite these findings, caregivers neither accessed nor sought mental health services for sizeable proportions of children estimated to have clinically significant mental health difficulties, namely 22% each of children with ACC (33/155) and CBCL (37/165) total scores in the respective clinical ranges, and 25% (48/189) of children with any CBCL sub-scale score in the clinical range. Failure to seek or access clinical services for these children was unrelated to the length of time they had spent in their present placements. Conversely, 39% each of children with non-problematic ACC (60/155) and CBCL (59/150) total scores had received one or more mental health services. The rates of mental health service use for children with various combinations of scores in the clinical ranges of the CBCL DSM-oriented scales are listed in Table 2.2.

These results in the CICS suggest that mental health service use is unrelated to broad typology of DSM-IV disorders (i.e. internalizing vs. externalizing vs. ADHD disorders). This contrasts with evidence elsewhere that children with attention-deficit/hyperactivity symptoms are more likely to receive specialist health services than children with other symptoms or disorders (Minnis et al., 2006; Zima et al., 2000) and that foster youth with conduct problems have greater difficulty accessing services, in some cases due to active exclusion of children with disruptive behaviours (Kerker & Dore, 2006). Instead, the CICS study found that children with greater symptom complexity and severity were more likely to access services, as indicated by clinical scores across two or more of the three typologies.

Table 2.2 Mental health service use by clinically significant CBCL DSM-oriented scores

Clinically significant DSM-oriented scores	N/347	Child individual therapy		Caregiver clinical guidance		Psychiatric medication	
		N	%	N	%	N	%
Internalizing DSM disorders only (Affective and/or Anxiety and/or Somatic)	27	13	48.2	16	59.3	1	3.7
Attention-deficit/hyperactivity only	9	2	22.2	3	33.3	2	22.2
Externalizing DSM disorders only (Conduct and/or Oppositional defiant)	58	31	53.5	31	53.5	12	20.7
Internalizing + ADHD, OR Internalizing + Externalizing	22	14	63.6	14	63.6	4	18.2
ADHD + Externalizing	30	19	63.3	19	63.3	8	26.7
Internalizing + ADHD + Externalizing	43	32	74.4	25	58.1	16	37.2

What other factors influence children's (and their caregivers') access to therapy and support?

Ethnicity

The relationship between children's ethnicity or minority status and their access to mental health services while in care is likely to vary across the western world. In the United States, while African American children in care may show a better match between symptom severity and use of services as compared to equivalent Caucasian children (Garland et al., 2000), they also have considerably less access to mental health services overall (Bellamy, 2007; Leslie, Hurlburt, Landsverk, Barth, & Slymen, 2004; Zima et al., 2000). Indeed, one study found that Caucasian children with a low level of emotional or behavioural difficulties were more likely to receive mental health services than children of other ethnicities with an intermediate level of difficulties (Garland et al., 2000).

Age

Older children in care are also more likely to receive mental health treatment (Bellamy, 2007), although we need to be mindful that older children in care have higher rates of mental health difficulties, including disruptive behaviour. In the CICS, it was found that older children were more likely to receive individual therapy, and this association held after controlling for children's mental health and other variables. Older children also had greater mental health problems, although this univariate age effect was confounded by children's age at entry into care (Tarren-Sweeney, 2008). Simply put, the greater mental health problems manifested by older children were largely accounted for by later entry into care, the latter being a strong predictor of mental health problems.

Gender

The relationship between gender and access to mental health services remains unclear because of conflicting and inconclusive findings (Bellamy, 2007; Blumberg et al., 1996; Burns et al., 2004). No gender differences were found in the CICS.

Maltreatment history

Several studies have found that active forms of maltreatment, most notably sexual abuse, predict higher use of mental health services after controlling for the scale of their mental health symptoms, while children who experience neglect are much less likely to receive services (Bellamy, 2007; Garland et al., 1996; Leslie et al., 2004). It is possible that children entering care following exposure to physical and sexual abuse are more likely to be routinely referred to mental health services for trauma-related treatment, regardless of their present mental health. However, in the CICS mental health service use was largely unrelated to the types of maltreatment children experienced. The single exception was that a confirmed history of emotional abuse predicted caregiver clinical guidance. The lack of other maltreatment effects on service use might be partly a function of the complexity of the maltreatment experienced by this Australian sample. It is questionable whether one can make valid distinctions between active forms of abuse and neglect among children with a background of severe, complex, and chronic maltreatment.

Placement-related factors

A number of factors relating to children's placement histories reportedly predict service use. There is some support for a behavioural service use model to explain caregiver decision-making in initiating and facilitating mental health services for children in care (Bellamy, 2007). Evidence from NSCAW also suggests that caregivers with higher educational background are more likely to seek and obtain services for children in their care, while controlling for ethnicity (Bellamy, 2007). Several placement-related variables that could feasibly impact on caregivers' willingness or ability to pursue services have not yet been adequately investigated, including caregiver age, the number of caregivers working outside the home, and the number of children in the home.

Placement stability

There are conflicting findings on the relationship between children's placement stability and their access to (and use of) mental health services. One recent study ($n = 570$) found that children with a history of disrupted placements (ostensibly as a consequence of their disruptive behaviour) had a higher rate of mental health service use than other children, after controlling for their mental health symptoms (James, Landsverk, Slymen, & Leslie, 2004). Their rate of service use increased markedly in the first three months following change of placement. However, another study found that children with greater placement instability were less likely to access treatment services (Zima et al., 2000).

Active casework

In the CICS, the sole predictor of total (i.e. *met* plus *unmet*) demand for mental health services was having an 'assigned caseworker'. At the time this survey was carried out in NSW, having an assigned caseworker was a marker for greater need for acute casework

support. Caseload pressures were such that children without critical or acute need for casework services were typically 'unassigned'
(i.e. not having an identified worker). Children receiving or in
need of mental health services are more likely to be viewed as
having acute need for services, such as interagency planning. Furthermore, their emotional or behavioural problems are more likely
to attract recognition of a need for casework support.

Structural and systemic barriers to child and adolescent mental health services

Active exclusion of children residing in statutory care from
CAMHS services is both widespread and long-standing. Wherever I go in the anglophone world, social workers describe much
the same discriminatory practices. The reasons given include
"The child's problems are behavioural, not psychiatric"; "The
young person doesn't meet diagnostic threshold . . . [or] . . .
Doesn't have a mental disorder" (despite the young person having complex symptomatology, and high functional impairment);
"The child has the wrong diagnosis" (e.g. exclusion of conduct
disorder); "The service doesn't have an evidence-based treatment
that can be matched to this child's formulation"; and "The service will only work with this young person if they are in a stable
placement".

The latter excuse can feel Kafkaesque for a social worker who
is trying to support a young person in psychological freefall in
the midst of serial placement breakdowns. Typically, a young
person in this situation experiences their exclusion from mental
health care amid a whirlwind of negative events. Disadvantage
thus builds on disadvantage, like compound interest. A recent par-
liamentary committee inquiring into mental health services for
children in statutory care in England highlighted several of these
practices. The committee recommended that CAMHS provide
priority access to children in statutory care, that they refrain from
excluding children who were without a stable placement, and
that this population's particular service needs be funded within
the health department's local child mental health plans (Local
Transformation Plans; House of Commons Education Committee, 2016). The committee did not directly address the question of

how additional funding for children in care can be found within existing NHS budgets, or alternatively, whether this warranted additional funding from central government. The developmental mechanisms that account for these children's complex symptomatology, as well as ongoing systemic pressures on their felt security, account for long recovery timeframes and questionable efficacy of standard treatments. Effective treatment of these problems undoubtedly requires more time and resources than present acute care service models allow. I think this is justified in light of the state's duty of care for our most vulnerable children, both from a moral viewpoint and a legal one – for many, the state is their legal guardian! But judicious investment in long-term mental health recovery for these children is also good economic policy. The costs incurred by government in caring for a child or young person with serial placement instability, as well as other costs that come from growing up without stable family support (e.g. youth justice costs), greatly outweigh the costs of sustaining that child in a placement made stable through intensive mental health treatment and support (Bazalgette, Rahilly, & Trevelyan, 2015; Ward, Holmes, & Soper, 2008).

But the exclusion practices listed above are not solely due to the present squeeze on resources that mental health services are facing around the world. They are also a natural consequence of the poor fit between traditional clinical training and practice models, and the complex clinical and social contexts that these children present to CAMHS. I should be clear in saying that these observations in the main apply to regular CAMHS services, not the small (but increasing) number of specialized CAMHS services that have been set up for these populations. I recently had the pleasure of spending 2 days with a new CAMHS service being established by the state health department in south-western Sydney, which is to be co-located with a child welfare office. While integration of specialist CAMHS services for children in care with statutory children's agencies is occurring in a number of locations (notably in the United Kingdom), this new Sydney service will support both children in care and higher risk maltreated children who are presently in their parents' care. In doing so, there is tacit recognition that these two vulnerable child populations require much the same specialized clinical skill set and a more flexible service model than that afforded by traditional CAMHS.

To be effective, these specialized services need to operate in ways that can support caregivers and children through long-term developmental recovery, that is abandoning the notion that an acute care service model can deliver effective treatment for children with complex attachment- and trauma-related psychopathology. They also require clinical staff with quite specialized knowledge and skill sets. I think it makes better sense to provide targeted training to those clinicians who elect to work in these specialized services than to attempt to up-skill clinicians across the board in attachment and trauma work. These specialized services are also more effective if they integrate closely with children's services, so that clinicians are part of the social care milieu. And finally, state or national networks of such specialized CAMHS services could finally provide decent access for those young people who are moved around the country due to placement instability.

The effectiveness of mental health interventions for children in alternative care

The rationale for providing mental health services to children in alternative care ultimately depends on the availability of mental health interventions that are meaningfully effective *for them*. Yet, among clinicians who work with these children, there is reasonable consensus that standard psychological and pharmacological interventions appear less effective for them. A U.S. study that examined mental health changes among a nationally representative sample of children in foster care identified some empirical support for this view. They found that outpatient mental health treatment had no independent effect on children's mental health over an 18-month period (Bellamy, Traube, & Gopalan, 2010) – suggesting that (collectively at least) interventions that constitute standard outpatient treatment in the United States may not be effective. Yet there is an increasing expectation that clinicians and mental health services working with children in care and adopted children should employ *evidence-based interventions* for treatment of disorders commonly diagnosed among these groups of children (Barth, Crea, John, Thoburn, & Quinton, 2005).

The current status of mental health interventions for children in care and those adopted from care

When considering the effectiveness of mental health interventions for referred children in care and adopted children, it is important to keep in mind that they are not a clinically homogenous group. At the very least, we need to separately consider treatment effectiveness for two broad clinical sub-populations described in Chapter 1, namely:

• Those children who have relatively non-complex psychopathology that can be reasonably formulated as discrete mental disorders or comorbidity using standard diagnostic classification (around 35% of the CICS cohort);
• Those children who present with complex attachment- and trauma-related psychopathology that is not adequately conceptualized within standard classification (around 20% of the CICS cohort; Tarren-Sweeney, 2013).

Whereas evidence gathered on the effectiveness of diagnosis-specific interventions from clinical trials with children at large have some relevance for the first group listed above, we should be less confident that such evidence can be generalized to the second group.

Types of mental health interventions

Mental health interventions are usually grouped according to the theoretical frameworks that guided their development, such as *behavioural, cognitive behavioural, psychodynamic*, and *systemic* psychotherapies. This approach is not particularly useful for the present purpose. For these children, we need to focus on multi-systemic interventions that involve multiple therapeutic mechanisms (particularly those explained by social learning, attachment, trauma, and systems theories). Instead, I think it is more useful to group mental health interventions for children in alternative care and their caregivers into the following categories:

1 *Primary prevention interventions* provided to children and young people exposed to specific adverse events or circumstances, which are designed to 'inoculate' them from new mental health symptoms, felt insecurity, or other adverse developmental

outcomes. Two examples of this are sexual abuse counselling provided to children following disclosure of sexual abuse, and life story work carried out with children who have complex care histories and/or disrupted attachments. In some instances these same interventions are prescribed to children after problems begin to emerge.

2   *Individual or group psychotherapy* targeting specific symptoms, disorders, or functioning. These are more commonly employed with older children and young people. Some examples include social skills training, trauma-focussed cognitive behaviour therapy (TF–CBT), dialectical behaviour therapy, and play therapy. In some cases individual psychotherapies are adapted to involve caregivers without necessarily employing a systemic focus.

3   *Systemic family/dyadic psychotherapies* that involve two or more individuals from a family or alternate family group. Some examples are family therapy, parent–child psychotherapy, attachment narrative therapy (Dallos & Dallos, 2013), and dyadic developmental psychotherapy (Hughes, 2004).

4   *Interventions primarily directed towards caregivers*, which aim to maximize caregiving as a primary therapeutic mechanism, and/or sustain children's placements. Examples include Attachment and Biobehavioral Catchup (Dozier, Bick, & Bernard, 2011), Parent Child Interaction Therapy (Timmer, Urquiza, & Zebell, 2006), Enhanced Adoptive Parenting (Rushton & Monck, 2009), and generic family behavioural interventions (such as Triple P, and Incredible Years).

5   *Multi-systemic/wraparound interventions* that target multiple components of a child's developmental ecology. These interventions simultaneously focus on reducing mental health symptoms (especially behavioural difficulties), strengthening close relationships, improving other functional outcomes (e.g. focussing on school education and peer socialization), and altering children's developmental pathways. The best-known example is Multidimensional Treatment Foster Care.

The specificity of interventions for children in alternative care

Some interventions are designed specifically for children in various forms of alternative care, such as Multidimensional Treatment

Foster Care for Preschoolers (MTFC-P; Fisher, Burraston, & Pears, 2005), Attachment and Biobehavioral Catchup, and Enhanced Adoptive Parenting. There are also some interventions that have been especially modified or adapted for use with these populations or their caregivers, such as attachment narrative therapy (Dallos & Dallos, 2013). However, most mental health interventions offered for these children and their caregivers are neither specifically designed nor modified for use with them. Sometimes these interventions are matched to children's symptoms or diagnoses, following guidance on evidence-based practice for children at large, without reference to symptom complexity or developmental context. There are few interventions that have been designed or modified to treat complex symptomatology, regardless of children's care status. However, efforts to modify dialectical behaviour therapy and metallization-based treatment (Midgley et al., 2017) for use with children and adolescents opens possibilities for more appropriate individual psychotherapies for children who have complex, trait-like symptomatology. Finally, some 'therapeutic' interventions and counselling are provided to children in care and adopted children without reference to a clinical formulation and without sufficient assessment data. Often this occurs when a therapist is trained in a single method, which they assume provides therapeutic benefits regardless of the type of difficulties a child presents with, or their developmental context.

Guidance from published reviews

There have been eight general reviews of mental health interventions for children and young people in statutory (out-of-home) care in recent years (Craven & Lee, 2006; Hambrick, Oppenheim-Weller, N'zi, & Taussig, 2016; Kinsey & Schlosser, 2013; Landsverk, Burns, Stambaugh, & Reutz, 2006, 2009; Leve et al., 2012; Luke, Sinclair, Woolgar, & Sebba, 2014; Racusin, Maerlender, Sengupta, Isquith, & Straus, 2005), as well as one relevant commentary (Barth et al., 2005) and one equivalent review for children adopted from care (Stock, Spielhofer, & Gieve, 2016). These reviews vary somewhat in their methodology, extent of systematic appraisal, how they rate treatment effectiveness, and conclusions.

Aside from published case reports, each of these reviews identified very few treatment studies carried out with children in care. It is notable that a small number of randomized controlled trials (RCTs) have been published more recently, which I describe later in this chapter. In lieu of effectiveness data that are specific to children in care, these reviews largely focus on the evidence base for treatments of mental health difficulties that commonly manifested among children in foster care (Landsverk et al., 2009), gathered from RCTs carried out with children at large. With a couple of exceptions, these reviews do not question the extent to which such data can be generalized to children in care, and adopted children. Some of the reviews do, however, refer to effectiveness data obtained for maltreated children, which holds greater validity for 'in care' and adopted children. Additionally, there have been several reviews on the effectiveness of specific types or classes of interventions, namely:

- Interventions for foster parents (Dorsey et al., 2008; Dozier, Albus, Fisher, & Sepulveda, 2002; Everson-Hock et al., 2012; Turner, MacDonald, & Dennis, 2009);
- Attachment-based support services and psychotherapies (Howe, 2006; Kerr & Cossar, 2014);
- Treatment models for group and residential care (James, 2011).

Guidance from organizations that promote evidence-based practice

Aside from published clinical reviews, clinicians and mental health services obtain guidance from various organizations and services that evaluate or translate the effectiveness of mental health interventions, including professional associations, research clearing houses, and organizations whose purpose is to identify and disseminate evidence-based practice – such as the U.K.'s National Institute for Health and Clinical Excellence (NICE). In recent years, a few such organizations have written about the particular mental health needs of children and young people in care (but not children adopted from care) – alluding mainly to the absence of an adequate evidence base and the need for further clinical effectiveness studies. A recent Faculty of Child and Adolescent

Psychiatry, Royal Australian and New Zealand College of Psychiatrists (RANZCP) report on the mental health needs of children and young people in care did not examine the effectiveness literature, but instead identified a critical shortfall in "clinical research into psychological and pharmacological treatment of the complex psychopathology of children in out-of-home care" (Royal Australian & New Zealand College of Psychiatrists, 2008, p. 39). NICE and the Social Care Institute for Excellence (SCIE) recently published a public health guideline for working with children and young people in care in the United Kingdom (NICE & SCIE, 2010). While the guideline neither reviews nor comments on treatment effectiveness, it recommended that government should fund and facilitate treatment effectiveness research for this population. Surprisingly, a set of research questions proposed in the guideline excluded any reference to identifying effective mental health interventions for this population – focussing instead on such things as social care models and access to mental health services. NICE has also published a number of clinical guidelines for treatment of child mental health difficulties, some of which are particularly pertinent to 'in care' and adopted children (notably ADHD, PTSD, conduct disorder, and depression). However, these guidelines do not examine differential treatment effectiveness for care populations or other vulnerable groups. In general, however, most clinical practice guidelines and treatment reviews published by professional associations to date, have not referred to treatment effectiveness for 'in care' or adopted children, or considered the extent to which efficacy findings generalize to special populations, or to children with complex difficulties (e.g. the Australian Psychological Society's review of evidence-based psychological interventions; Australian Psychological Society, 2010).

Presently, the most authoritative guidance on mental health interventions for child welfare clients (including those residing in care and those adopted from care) is provided by the California Evidence-Based Clearinghouse for Child Welfare (funded by the state child welfare department). The clearinghouse reviews the effectiveness of mental health interventions in terms of:

1 *Scientific rating*: Based on classical efficacy/effectiveness data from clinical trials. The scientific rating has a 5-point scale

ranging from 'I. well-supported by research evidence' to 'V. concerning practice';

2   *Child welfare system relevance level*: The extent to which the intervention is either purposely designed for child welfare clients and/or has been trialled with child welfare samples. Child welfare system relevance levels are *high, medium* or *low*.

Findings from clinical treatment trials

As mentioned previously in this chapter, there has been little substantive research into the effectiveness and appropriateness of mental health interventions for children in care and adopted children, either through examining therapy process or therapeutic outcomes. This is not to say that interventions for these populations have not been developed, or that they are ineffective. Rather, most promising interventions have yet to be adequately evaluated. In this section, research findings from five interventions that have been evaluated in clinical trials are summarized and discussed.

Multidimensional Treatment Foster Care

Multidimensional Treatment Foster Care (MTFC) is an intensive, wraparound, multi-component intervention in which children and young people reside for a limited time period with a *treatment* foster family (Chamberlain, 2003). It was initially developed as an alternative to residential and group care for adolescent young offenders and those with severe behavioural and emotional problems, and to date has largely been studied with participants who otherwise would be placed in residential treatment (and would not necessarily be residing in alternative care; MacDonald & Turner, 2008). Evaluation trials have largely been carried out with populations of high-risk young people who, aside from the fostering intervention, were not otherwise growing up in alternative care. Nevertheless, its success with these other high-risk youth suggests some potential for use with young people in the care system whose disruptiveness generates placement instability, who have complex mental health difficulties, and who otherwise are more likely to be placed in residential care.

To date, only one research trial of MTFC has been carried out with older children and young people already residing in alternative care. This recent U.K. study consisted of parallel RCT and observational investigations, with most participants being enrolled in the latter study (aged 11–16, N = 219; Biehal et al., 2012). Propensity score matching was employed to adjust for differences between the quasi-experimental and control (usual foster care) samples. Importantly, the treatment and control samples were young people who had unstable placement histories and had either been in residential care or were on a pathway to residential care. Following propensity score matching, participants who received MTFC did not significantly differ from the control group on a range of outcomes, including subsequent placement stability, participation in education, or recorded offending, and pre-post changes in global functioning (CGAS) and mental health (CBCL, SDQ, HoNOSCA, DAWBA-AD; Biehal et al., 2012). Young people who had serious antisocial behaviour problems did better if they resided in MTFC, while those who were not seriously antisocial did better in regular care. It was notable that many of the latter group had mental health difficulties other than antisocial behaviour. These findings suggest that MTFC may be effective for older children and young people in the care system who are seriously antisocial and who do not have complex mental health difficulties.

Multidimensional Treatment Foster Care for Preschoolers

Multidimensional Treatment Foster Care for Preschoolers (MTFC-P) and Early Intervention Foster Care (EIFC) are variations of MTFC adapted for children in care aged 3–6 years who have yet to obtain permanent placements (Fisher, Gunnar, Chamberlain, & Reid, 2000). It is unclear whether EIFC and MTFC-P differ in any substantial way, or if the intervention that was previously called EIFC was later renamed MTFC-P. Whereas MTFC is designed for children with existing mental health difficulties, MTFC-P is a preventative, population-based intervention for preschool-aged children in care. The MTFC-P contains a number of developmentally informed variations from MTFC that make it more appropriate for preschool-aged children. The "intervention is delivered via a team approach to the child, foster care provider, and permanent placement resource (birth parents and adoptive relatives or non-relatives)" (Fisher et al., 2005, p.65). A goal of the intervention is to transition children to a permanent placement, typically involving 6–9 months (Fisher et al., 2005).

An RCT carried out by the intervention developers[1] demonstrated several important findings that suggest MTFC-P is an efficacious intervention for such children. Compared with preschoolers residing in regular temporary foster care (the control intervention), children placed with MTFC-P caregivers showed significant increases in secure attachment behaviour and reductions in insecure avoidant attachment behaviour over the study period (Fisher & Kim, 2007). By the end of the treatment period, they also manifested stress hormone activity patterns resembling those of non-maltreated children at large, whereas the control sample continued to show abnormal stress hormone activity consistent with their early history of maltreatment (Fisher et al., 2000). Among a sub-sample of children who entered the study with unstable placement histories ($N = 52$), children in a MTFC-P placement had double the rate of retention within their subsequent permanent placements 2 years post-study than control children (Fisher, Kim, & Pears, 2009). Except for the stability of subsequent permanent placements, these effects were measured while the participants were in the care of their treatment and regular foster parents. Otherwise, the effects of children being moved to a subsequent placement, including any effects of loss of attachment figures, could not be measured using this particular study design, as both the treatment and control samples experienced a subsequent change of placement.

MTFC-P is a particularly promising intervention for young children with mental health difficulties and prior placement instability who would otherwise have required a further temporary placement prior to obtaining permanency. It perhaps has the potential to stabilize children in such circumstances and to increase their chances of attaining non-disrupted permanent care. Given such demonstrated benefits, I think it is important to guard against seeing MTFC-P as necessary preparation for permanency for young children in care who have serious behaviour problems, if the implication is that their time in temporary foster care is extended (see discussion about the developmental appropriateness of extended temporary care at the end of this chapter).

KEEP

Whereas MTFC and MTFC-P involve active placement of a single child or young person with specially trained treatment foster parents (with no other child residing in the home), elements of MTFC have also been modified and applied as a more naturalistic intervention designed to support existing foster and kinship placements, called KEEP (keeping foster and kinship parents trained and supported; Price, Chamberlain, Landsverk, & Reid, 2009). KEEP is a less radical intervention than MTFC for many children already residing in care because it does not require a change of placement when treatment is completed, and it is also designed to support placements that have more than one child. Therefore, KEEP can be offered without disrupting existing relationships with long-term or permanent caregivers and co-placed siblings.

The effectiveness of the KEEP intervention has been evaluated in a large RCT that compared outcomes for children in foster and kinship care (ages 5–12 years, $N = 700$) randomly allocated to either the KEEP programme or to continue receiving standard casework services (that included some training for caregivers; Price et al., 2009). It is unclear whether this study measured access to other mental health services or interventions by control children during the study period. Children whose caregivers received the KEEP intervention showed a modest although meaningful pre-post intervention reduction in their mean number of behaviour problems per day (reduced from 5.9 to 4.4), whereas the group who received usual care showed less meaningful reduction (5.8–5.4; Chamberlain et al., 2008). Furthermore, the biggest reductions in behaviour problems were observed among those children who had higher levels of initial problems. The other critical finding was that children in the KEEP-supported placements were more likely to obtain a planned move to a permanent placement (i.e. restoration, permanent kinship placement, or adoption) than control children (Price et al., 2008). However, there was no difference between the groups in the rate of unplanned placement breakdowns and other negative exits from children's current placements. A more recent RCT measured similarly modest reductions in children's behaviour problems across the treatment period for those children who were the focus of treatment, but also measured behavioural improvements among their siblings, suggesting that KEEP has a therapeutic effect on all children residing in the home (Price, Roesch, Walsh, & Landsverk, 2015). A recent English trial of KEEP was hampered by a lack of a control group but nonetheless provided encouraging signs that therapeutic benefits are maintained 12 months post-intervention *for those children who remain in placement*, as well as tentative evidence that the study group enjoyed greater 12-month placement stability than is otherwise the case for children in foster care who are in need of mental health interventions or support (Roberts, Glynn, & Waterman, 2016).

Attachment and Biobehavioral Catchup (ABC)

The ABC intervention was developed by Mary Dozier and her colleagues to facilitate relationship formation and associated biobehavioural developmental for maltreated infants and toddlers, and for those who have experienced disrupted attachments. The intervention was evaluated in an RCT with a sample of infants and toddlers in foster care, where the control intervention was provision of developmental education. Published findings were derived from a number of different analyses carried out at different stages of participant recruitment, with the number of study participants ranging from 46 to 93, with half of those numbers being randomly allocated to each of the ABC and control interventions. In the first analysis, treatment infants ($N = 23$) showed significantly less avoidant attachment behaviour than control infants following distress-eliciting incidents reported over a 3-day period (Dozier et al., 2009). However, this analysis does not appear to take into account infants' pre-treatment attachment security. In the second set of analyses, the distribution of post-intervention morning and afternoon cortisol production by treatment infants ($N = 30$) closely paralleled that of a comparison sample of infants at large who were not in foster care ($N = 104$), and was significantly lower than that produced by control infants (Dozier et al., 2006). Moreover, the difference in mean cortisol production between treatment and control infants was developmentally significant. While treatment and control infants manifested a similar scale of post-intervention behaviour problems, an age effect was found among the treatment sample – with treated toddlers (18–36 months) having fewer behaviour problems than treated infants. In the third set of analyses, treatment infants ($N = 46$) showed considerably lower stress reactions than control infants during a strange situation procedure, as measured by cortisol production (measured before, and then 15 and 30 minutes after the procedure; Dozier, Peloso, Lewis, Laurenceau, & Levine, 2008). An important additional finding was that infants receiving the ABC intervention had very similar cortisol levels at each point of measurement to an additional comparison sample ($N = 48$) of infants at large who were not in foster care, suggesting their stress regulation is normatively distributed. A more recent article reports that 44 foster mothers who received the ABC intervention showed greater improvement in sensitivity towards their foster infants than did 52 foster mothers who received a control intervention (Bick & Dozier, 2013); the article does not state if this is the same treatment cohort as described in previous articles, or if this is a new study cohort.

In summary, there is good evidence that the ABC intervention has a therapeutic effect on the stress regulation and attachment security of infants and toddlers in care, but inconclusive evidence that this translates into reduced behaviour problems shortly after treatment. It is important to note that achieving normalization of infant stress regulation and increased attachment security has far greater developmental significance for subsequent mental health than reducing their frequency of behaviour problems.

Comparison of three trauma symptom interventions

The effectiveness of three age-bounded interventions designed to treat traumatic stress symptoms was evaluated in a clinical trial with 133 children and young people (aged 3–18) enrolled in a wraparound foster care programme in the United States who had previously experienced a moderate or severely traumatic incident (Weiner, Schneider, & Lyons, 2009). The interventions were Child–Parent Psychotherapy (CPP, $N = 65$, ages 3–6), Trauma-Focussed Cognitive Behavioural Therapy (TF-CBT, $N = 35$, ages 3–16), and Structured Psychotherapy for Adolescents Responding to Chronic Stress (SPARCS, $N = 33$, ages 13–18). The goal of CPP is to facilitate young (ages 0–5) children's recovery from traumatic stress by increasing parental sensitivity, strengthening parent–child attachments, and boosting children's felt security using a dyadic psychotherapy format. The extent of children's direct engagement in CPP varies according to their age. TF–CBT attempts to reduce children's unpleasant physiological trauma symptoms using a range of cognitive, behavioural, and psycho-education techniques. While the child is the primary participant in TF–CBT, the intervention includes education for parents that seeks to normalize their child's experiences, moderate unhelpful parental reactions to their child's distress, and provide emotional support for their child. SPARCS is a group intervention for adolescents who have been exposed to traumatic stressors. It employs various components of dialectical behaviour therapy with strong focus on acquiring improved mindfulness, interpersonal skills, and coping abilities. Each of these interventions had previously been evaluated with traumatized children at large.

The study design did not include a control intervention, although inclusion of three study interventions provided opportunity to compare their relative effectiveness. The study's primary goal was to identify the relative effectiveness of these interventions with different racial groups. Treatment effect sizes were not reported for the aggregate samples, and some of the ethnicity treatment groups had too few participants to estimate treatment effectiveness. Clinically meaningful pre-post reductions in trauma symptoms were measured for young African American, biracial, and Hispanic (but not white) children who received CPP. Clinically meaningful reductions were measured for African American and white children who received TF–CBT (no other ethnicity group had sufficient sample size). African American youth who participated in the SPARCS intervention showed a statistically significant, although less clinically meaningful reduction in trauma symptoms (other ethnic groups had insufficient sample size). These results were achieved in a real-world setting and thus can be considered to be measures of effectiveness. The study findings suggest that CPP and TF–CBT are possibly effective interventions for treatment of trauma symptoms experienced by children in care, while SPARCS is a less promising intervention for young people in care.

Note

[1] I have assumed that various study publications dating from 2000 to 2009 refer to a single RCT carried out in Oregon, reporting various analyses carried out at different stages of sample recruitment. However, the publications may instead be referring to two separate RCTs.

References

Australian Psychological Society. (2010). *Evidence-based psychological interventions in the treatment of mental disorders: A literature review* (3rd ed.). Melbourne: Australian Psychological Society.

Barth, R., Crea, T., John, K., Thoburn, J., & Quinton, D. (2005). Beyond attachment theory and therapy: Towards sensitive and evidence-based interventions with foster and adoptive families in distress. *Child and Family Social Work, 10*, 257–268.

Bazalgette, L., Rahilly, T. & Trevelyan, G. (2015). *Achieving emotional wellbeing for looked after children: a whole system approach.* London: NSPCC.

Bellamy, J. (2007). *Mental health need, outpatient service use, and outcomes among children who have experienced long-term foster care.* Dissertation, Columbia University, New York.

Bellamy, J., Traube, D., & Gopalan, G. (2010). A national study of the impact of outpatient mental health services for children in long-term foster care. *Clinical Child Psychology and Psychiatry, 15*(4), 467–480.

Bick, J., & Dozier, M. (2013). The effectiveness of an attachment-based intervention in promoting foster mothers' sensitivity toward foster infants. *Infant Mental Health Journal, 34*(2), 95–103.

Biehal, N., Dixon, J., Parry, E., Sinclair, I., Green, J., Roberts, C., . . . Roby, A. (2012). *The Care Placements Evaluation (CAPE): Evaluation of Multidimensional Treatment Foster Care for Adolescents (MTFC-A).* London: Department for Education.

Blumberg, E., Landsverk, J., Ellis-MacLeod, E., Ganger, W., et al. (1996). Use of the public mental health system by children in foster care: Client characteristics and service use patterns. *Journal of Mental Health Administration, 23*(4), 389–405.

Burns, B., Phillips, S., Wagner, H., Barth, R., Kolko, D., Campbell, Y., & Landsverk, J. (2004). Mental health need and access to mental health services by youths involved with child welfare: A national survey. *Journal of the American Academy of Child & Adolescent Psychiatry, 43*(8), 960–970.

Chamberlain, P. (2003). The Oregon Multidimensional Treatment Foster Care model: Features, outcomes, and progress in dissemination. *Cognitive and Behavioral Practice, 10*, 303–312.

Chamberlain, P., Price, J., Leve, L., Laurent, H., Landsverk, J., & Reid, J. (2008). Prevention of behavior problems for children in foster care: Outcomes and mediation effects. *Prevention Science, 9*, 17–27.

Children and Young Persons (Care and Protection) Act 1998 No 157 (NSW).

Craven, P., & Lee, R. (2006). Therapeutic interventions for foster children: A systematic research synthesis. *Research on Social Work Practice, 16*(3), 287–304.

Dallos, R., & Dallos, A. (2013). Using an attachment narrative approach with families where the children are looked after or adopted. In M. Tarren-Sweeney & A. Vetere (Eds.), *Mental health services for vulnerable children and young people: Supporting children who are, or have been, in foster care*. London: Routledge.

Dorsey, S., Farmer, E., Barth, R., Greene, K., Reid, J., & Landsverk, J. (2008). Current status and evidence base of training for foster and treatment foster parents. *Children & Youth Services Review, 30*, 1403–1416.

Dozier, M., Albus, K., Fisher, P., & Sepulveda, S. (2002). Interventions for foster parents: Implications for developmental theory. *Development and Psychopathology, 14*, 843–860.

Dozier, M., Bick, J., & Bernard, K. (2011). Attachment-based treatment for young, vulnerable children. In J. Osofsky & A. Lieberman (Eds.), *Clinical work with traumatized young children*. New York, NY: Guilford Press.

Dozier, M., Lindheim, O., Lewis, E., Bick, J., Bernard, K., & Peloso, E. (2009). Effects of a foster parent training program on young children's attachment behaviors: Preliminary evidence from a randomized clinical trial. *Child and Adolescent Social Work Journal, 26*, 321–332.

Dozier, M., Peloso, E., Lewis, E., Laurenceau, J., & Levine, S. (2008). Effects of an attachment-based intervention on the cortisol production of infants and toddlers in foster care. *Development and Psychopathology, 20*, 845–859.

Dozier, M., Peloso, E., Lindheim, O., Gordon, M. K., Manni, M., Sepulveda, S., & Ackerman, J. (2006). Developing evidence-based interventions for foster children: An example of a randomized clinical trial with infants and toddlers. *Journal of Social Issues, 62*(4), 767–785.

Everson-Hock, E., Jones, R., Guillaume, L., Clapton, J., Goyder, E., Chilcott, J., . . . Swann, C. (2012). The effectiveness of training and support for carers and other professionals on the physical and emotional health and well-being of looked-after children and young people: A systematic review. *Child: Care, Health & Development, 38*(2), 162–174.

Fisher, P. A., Burraston, B., & Pears, K. (2005). The Early Intervention Foster Care program: Permanent placement outcomes from a randomized trial. *Child Maltreatment, 10*(1), 61–71.

Fisher, P. A., Gunnar, M., Chamberlain, P., & Reid, J. (2000). Preventive intervention for maltreated preschool children: Impact on children's behavior, neuroendocrine activity, and foster parent functioning. *Journal of the American Academy of Child & Adolescent Psychiatry, 39*(11), 1356.

Fisher, P. A., & Kim, H. (2007). Intervention effects on foster preschoolers' attachment-related behaviors from a randomized trial. *Prevention Science, 8,* 161–170.

Fisher, P. A., Kim, H., & Pears, K. (2009). Effects of Multidimensional Treatment Foster Care for Preschoolers (MTFC-P) on reducing permanent placement failures among children with placement instability. *Children and Youth Services Review, 31,* 541–546.

Garland, A., Hough, R., Landsverk, J., McCabe, K., Yeh, M., Ganger, W., & Reynolds, B. (2000). Racial and ethnic variations in mental health care utilization among children in foster care. *Children's Services: Social Policy, Research, and Practice, 3*(3), 133–146.

Garland, A., Landsverk, J., Hough, R., & Ellis-Macleod, E. (1996). Type of maltreatment as a predictor of mental health service use for children in foster care. *Child Abuse & Neglect, 20*(8), 675–688.

Hambrick, E., Oppenheim-Weller, S., N'zi, A., & Taussig, H. (2016). Mental health interventions for children in foster care: A systematic review. *Children & Youth Services Review, 70,* 65–77.

Hazell, P., & Stuart, J. (2003). A randomized controlled trial of Clonidine added to psychostimulant medication for hyperactive and aggressive children. *Journal of the American Academy of Child & Adolescent Psychiatry, 42*(8), 886–894.

House of Commons Education Committee. (2016). *Mental health and well-being of looked-after children: Fourth report of session 2015–16.* London: UK Parliament.

Howe, D. (2006). Developmental attachment psychotherapy with fostered and adopted children. *Child & Adolescent Mental Health, 11*(3), 128–134.

Hughes, D. (2004). An attachment-based treatment for maltreated children and young people. *Attachment and Human Development, 6*(3), 263–278.

James, S. (2011). What works in group care? A structured review of treatment models for group homes and residential care. *Children and Youth Services Review, 33*(2), 308–321.

James, S., Landsverk, J., Slymen, D. J., & Leslie, L. K. (2004). Predictors of outpatient mental health service use: The role of foster care placement change. *Mental Health Services Research, 6*(3), 127–141.

Kerker, B., & Dore, M. (2006). Mental health needs and treatment of foster youth: Barriers and opportunities. *American Journal of Orthopsychiatry, 76*(1), 138–147.

Kerr, L., & Cossar, J. (2014). Attachment interventions with foster and adoptive parents: A systematic review. *Child Abuse Review, 23,* 426–439.

Kinsey, D., & Schlosser, A. (2013). Interventions in foster and kinship care: A systematic review. *Clinical Child Psychology & Psychiatry, 18*(3), 429–463.

Landsverk, J., Burns, B., Stambaugh, L., & Reutz, J. (2006). Mental health care for children and adolescents in foster care: Review of research literature: Casey Family Programs.

Landsverk, J., Burns, B., Stambaugh, L., & Reutz, J. (2009). Psychosocial interventions for children and adolescents in foster care: Review of research literature. *Child Welfare*, *88*(1), 49–69.

Leslie, L., Hurlburt, M., James, S., Landsverk, J., Slymen, D. J., & Zhang, J. (2005). Relationship between entry into child welfare and mental health service use. *Psychiatric Services*, *56*(8), 981–987.

Leslie, L., Hurlburt, M., Landsverk, J., Barth, R. P., & Slymen, D. J. (2004). Outpatient mental health services for children in foster care: A national perspective. *Child Abuse & Neglect*, *28*, 697–712.

Leslie, L., Landsverk, J., Ezzet-Lofstrom, R., Tschann, J. M., Slymen, D. J., & Garland, A. F. (2000). Children in foster care: Factors influencing outpatient mental health service use. *Child Abuse & Neglect*, *24*(4), 465–476.

Leve, L., Harold, G., Chamberlain, P., Landsverk, J., Fisher, P., & Vostanis, P. (2012). Practitioner review: Children in foster care: Vulnerabilities and evidence-based interventions that promote resilience processes. *Journal of Child Psychology & Psychiatry*, *53*(12), 1197–1211.

Luke, N., Sinclair, I., Woolgar, M., & Sebba, J. (2014). *What works in preventing and treating poor mental health in looked after children?* Oxford: University of Oxford Department of Education.

MacDonald, G., & Turner, W. (2008). Treatment foster care for improving outcomes in children and young people (Review): Cochrane Collaboration.

Midgley, N., Besser, S., Dye, H., Fearon, P., Gale, T., Jefferies-Sewell, K., . . . Wood, S. (2017). The Herts and minds study: Evaluating the effectiveness of Mentalization-Based Treatment (MBT) as an intervention for children in foster care with emotional and/or behavioural problems: A phase II, feasibility, randomised controlled trial. *Pilot and Feasibility Studies*, *3*(12).

Minnis, H., Everett, K., Pelosi, A., Dunn, J., & Knapp, M. (2006). Children in foster care: Mental health, service use and costs. *European Child and Adolescent Psychiatry*, *15*, 63–70.

National Survey of Child and Adolescent Well-Being. (2003). One year in foster care: Wave 1 data analysis report. Retrieved August 2008 from www.acf.hhs.gov/programs/opre/abuse_neglect/nscaw/reports/nscaw_oyfc/oyfc_report.pdf

NICE, & SCIE. (2010). *Promoting the quality of life of looked-after children and young people: Public health guidance PH28*. London: NICE and SCIE.

Price, J., Chamberlain, P., Landsverk, J., & Reid, J. (2009). KEEP foster-parent training intervention: Model description and effectiveness. *Child and Family Social Work*, *14*, 233–242.

Price, J., Chamberlain, P., Landsverk, J., Reid, J., Leve, L., & Laurent, H. (2008). Effects of a foster parent training intervention on placement changes of children in foster care. *Child Maltreatment, 13*(1), 64–75.

Price, J., Roesch, S., Walsh, N., & Landsverk, J. (2015). Effects of the KEEP foster parent intervention on child and sibling behavior problems and parental stress during a randomized implementation trial. *Prevention Science, 16*, 685–695.

Racusin, R., Maerlender, A., Sengupta, A., Isquith, P., & Straus, M. (2005). Psychosocial treatment of children in foster care: A review. *Community Mental Health Journal, 41*(2), 199–221.

Roberts, R., Glynn, G., & Waterman, C. (2016). 'We know it works but does it last?' The implementation of the KEEP foster and kinship carer training programme in England. *Adoption & Fostering, 40*(3), 247–263.

Royal Australian & New Zealand College of Psychiatrists. (2008). *The mental health care needs of children in out-of-home care: A report from the expert working committee of the Faculty of Child and Adolescent Psychiatry.* Melbourne: RANZCP.

Rushton, A., & Monck, E. (2009). *Enhancing adoptive parenting.* London: BAAF.

Sawyer, M., Carbone, J., Searle, A., & Robinson, P. (2007). The mental health and well-being of children and adolescents in home-based foster care. *Medical Journal of Australia, 186*, 181–184.

Stock, L., Spielhofer, T., & Gieve, M. (2016). *Independent evidence review of post-adoption support interventions.* London: Department for Education. Retrieved from www.gov.uk/government/publications/post-adoption-support-interventions-independent-evidence-review.

Sturgess, W., & Selwyn, J. (2007). Supporting the placements of children adopted out of care. *Clinical Child Psychology and Psychiatry, 12*(1), 13–28.

Tarren-Sweeney, M. (2008). Retrospective and concurrent predictors of the mental health of children in care. *Children & Youth Services Review, 30*, 1–25.

Tarren-Sweeney, M. (2010). Concordance of mental health impairment and service utilisation among children in care. *Clinical Child Psychology and Psychiatry, 15*(4), 481–495.

Tarren-Sweeney, M. (2013). An investigation of complex attachment- and trauma-related symptomatology among children in foster and kinship care. *Child Psychiatry & Human Development, 44*, 727–741.

Timmer, S., Urquiza, A., & Zebell, N. (2006). Challenging foster caregiver-maltreated child relationships: The effectiveness of parent-child interaction therapy. *Children and Youth Services Review, 28*, 1–19.

Turner, W., MacDonald, G., & Dennis, J. (2009). Behavioural and cognitive behavioural training interventions for assisting foster carers in the management of difficult behaviour (Review): Cochrane Collaboration.

Ward, H., Holmes, L., & Soper, J. (2008). *Costs and consequences of placing children in care.* London: Jessica Kingsley.

Weiner, D., Schneider, A., & Lyons, J. (2009). Evidence-based treatments for trauma among culturally diverse foster care youth: Treatment retention and outcomes. *Children and Youth Services Review, 31,* 1199–1205.

Zima, B. T., Bussing, R., Yang, X., & Belin, T. R. (2000). Help-seeking steps and service use for children in foster care. *Journal of Behavioral Health Services & Research, 27*(3), 271–285.

3   Brief assessment, screening, and monitoring – what's the difference, and does it matter?

Demystifying brief assessment, screening, and monitoring

One of my reasons for writing this book is to help children's agencies develop a clear understanding of what types of mental health assessment should be provided to children under their supervision. This includes understanding what it is that agencies can do themselves 'in house' without clinical oversight, as well as demystifying the nature of screening and assessment carried out by clinical services. The book aims to empower agencies with knowledge that they need to advocate for clinical services on behalf of the children they have responsibility for, as well as their foster parents and adoptive parents. This of course has potential political and public policy implications. If agencies have a clearer understanding of which and how many children in alternative care require therapeutic services, then any shortfall in the availability of children's mental health services is less likely to be swept under the carpet.

Screening carried out by clinical services such as public CAMHS is often calibrated to match the service's intake capacity, rather than objectively identifying children and their families who are likely to require therapeutic services. In this context, the term 'screening' is misapplied. It is not screening in the true sense of the word – rather it is a form of *triage*. Unfortunately, over time the belief can arise that if a child is not accepted for a service following a screening assessment, then the child doesn't have clinical-level difficulties. Aside from the implications this has for the child's future development and well-being, being told that a child doesn't have serious-enough difficulties to warrant clinical support can be very distressing for foster parents and adoptive parents, as well as for children's social workers. Indeed, I think that when foster parents in particular feel that their experiences of a child's difficulties are de-legitimized, they can feel abandoned by the state, and the risk of placement breakdown increases.

Correct *versus* loosely applied *terminology*

The term 'screening' is often loosely applied in the child and adolescent mental health field. The word has three different connotations:

1   First, it can refer to screening in the proper sense of the word, namely use of a brief assessment tool or protocol that has good sensitivity for detecting children that have clinical-level difficulties, followed by more detailed assessment of positive screens.

2   Second, the word 'screening' is often incorrectly used as a synonym for 'brief', 'short', or 'quick' – as in a screening assessment is one that is brief. This extends to how we think about brief psychometric measures or brief interviews. These are often referred to as 'screening measures' or 'screening interviews'. However, if you were to ask clinicians why they use these 'screening' measures or interviews, their answers would rarely refer to screening principles. Rather, they identify a need for an assessment measure that can be administered quickly and requires little interpretation.

3   Third, the term 'screening assessment' is used in this field to describe initial intake assessments. These typically follow a prescribed format, are applied to all new referrals, tend to be questionnaire-driven, and tend not to require high-level clinical reasoning. These are brief, routine initial assessment protocols that are designed to act as a gateway to the service, or as a form of triage. Where these protocols differ from orthodox screening protocols is that they are designed to be more

specific than *sensitive* in detecting children who need clinical services (sensitivity and specificity are explained on the following pages). Second, the decision to accept or decline a referral is typically made at this initial assessment stage, not following further assessment, as occurs in classic multi-stage screening.

These loose applications of the word 'screening' in the child and adolescent mental health field are, I think, partly due to brief assessment measures being designed for multiple purposes, including (1) screening (in the proper sense of the word), (2) brief assessment, and (3) mental health monitoring, such as for assessing treatment effectiveness, or generating service-wide administrative data. The SDQ is ubiquitous in this regard, particularly in the United Kingdom where it was developed. Its developer correctly states that "the SDQ can be used for screening, as part of a clinical assessment, as a treatment-outcome measure, and as a research tool" (Goodman, 2001, p. 1337). Yet many clinicians who use the SDQ do not consciously differentiate these different tasks. They may use the SDQ in their regular assessments; SDQs may also be routinely gathered by their service for administrative purposes; and they may use the SDQ to monitor treatment progress. Yet in each of these contexts clinicians often refer to the SDQ as a 'screening' tool.

Understanding mental health screening: principles and statistics

Mental health *assessment* is expensive, it can be intrusive, and it needs to be carried out by professionals with a high level of clinical training. While mental health *screening* is less accurate than assessment at identifying children who have need for clinical services, it is more cost-effective, less intrusive, and does not need to be administered by mental health professionals. The decision to employ population-based health screening, as well as the overall screening strategy that is adopted, requires some understanding of the trade-off between accuracy on the one hand and efficiency and societal impact on the other.

Screening versus assessment

In general, the less common a health problem is, the less appropriate it is to subject an entire population to assessment of it. The population prevalence of autism is around 2% for boys and 0.5% for girls. Even though autism is a very serious developmental condition, and early detection and intervention can manifestly improve children's subsequent development and well-being, most people would generally agree that it would be inappropriate to subject *all* young children to formal assessment for autism. First of all, the cost would be prohibitive. Second, we could not justify intrusive assessment of all children (which would involve their parents as well) when more than 98% of them do not have the condition. Third, it would generate a lot of unnecessary concern among parents. At the other extreme are the populations covered by this book among whom the prevalence of mental disorders is greater than 50%. It is this exceptional prevalence rate that drives my argument in Chapter 6 to replace mental health screening with universal comprehensive psychological assessment of children in statutory care.

Screening terminology and concepts

The goal of mental health screening is to accurately differentiate between people who have clinical-level mental health difficulties and those who do not. The medical model conceptualizes health problems in terms of the presence or absence of morbidity, such that a person is seen as either having a disorder or not. The rationale for screening is based on the premise that one's disease status has just two values: we either have a disease or we do not. Of course, those of you who work closely with children in alternative care will understand that their mental health difficulties are manifested on a continuum (statisticians call this a 'continuously distributed variable'), rather than fitting neatly into either being a mental disorder or not. Nevertheless, when we are faced with the question of whether or not to refer a child for clinical assessment, or for some type of intervention or treatment, our own actions are typically dichotomous – we either make the referral or we do not. So I believe that the concept of screening remains practically useful, in spite of the fact that fitting children's mental health difficulties into just two categories is somewhat artificial.

For the purposes of screening, children who have clinical-level mental health difficulties are referred to as *cases*, and children who do not have clinical-level difficulties are referred to as *non-cases*. Because the goal of screening is to accurately differentiate between cases and non-cases, a screening measure is designed to yield two possible values. One value predicts that a person has a disorder or disease. We refer to this as a *positive* screen. In other words, if a child has a score on a screening measure that falls within the range of scores that predict the presence of morbidity, then they are said to have screened positive for that morbidity. Conversely, if a child has a score on a screening measure that falls outside the range of scores that predict the presence of morbidity, then they are said to have screened *negative* on that measure.

All screening concepts and statistics are concerned with the rates of concordance between children's disease status (i.e. *case* vs. *non-case*) and their screening result (i.e. *positive screen* vs. *negative screen*). The four possible combinations of screening result and disease status are described in the following way:

Cases who screen *positive* are	*True Positives*
Cases who screen *negative* are	*False Negatives*
Non-cases who screen *positive* are	*False Positives*
Non-cases who screen *negative* are	*True Negatives*

Remember that the goal of screening is to accurately differentiate between cases and non-cases. A perfect screening measure would thus only have true positives and true negatives (there would be no false identifications). Therefore, one way to judge the accuracy of a screening measure is to look at the rates of screening decisions that fall into each of these four categories:

> The *true positive* rate is the proportion of all cases who screen positive, and is referred to as the *sensitivity* rate. This rate describes how *sensitive* a measure is at detecting cases – or for the purposes of this book, children who have clinical-level mental health difficulties.

The *true negative* rate is the proportion of all non-cases who screen negative, and is referred to as the *specificity* rate. This rate describes how *specific* a measure is – in terms of its accuracy in excluding non-cases from further inquiry.

	Cases (Children who have problems)	Non-cases (Children without problems)
Positive screen	True Positives	False Positives
Negative screen	False Negatives	True Negatives

Screening accuracy and utility

If the goal of screening is to accurately differentiate between cases and non-cases, then this can only be achieved by maximizing *both* sensitivity and specificity. At this stage it is important to note that a screening measure doesn't have a single sensitivity rate and a single specificity rate. Mental health screening measures are typically checklists consisting of multiple items in which the individual item scores are summed to yield one or more total scores. These total scores thus tend to have a large range of possible values. For example, the SDQ total difficulties score ranges from zero to 40, with higher scores indicating greater mental health difficulties. On problem measures such as the SDQ, we define positive screens as all scores that fall at or above a defined score, called the *cut-point score*, while negative screens are all scores that fall below the cut-point score. A screening measure's accuracy is often described in terms of a single pair of sensitivity and specificity rates, which apply to the measure's recommended cut-point. This is somewhat misleading, as it suggests that a screening measure's accuracy can be ascertained solely from these two statistics. In fact, every score on a screening measure is a potential cut-point that has its own set of sensitivity and specificity rates. A screening measure's accuracy is not indicated by the sensitivity and specificity rates for the preferred cut-point; it is indicated by the sensitivity and specificity rates obtained for all potential cut-points. The way that this is done is to plot the true positive (sensitivity) rate on the *y*-axis against the false positive (1 ¬specificity) rate on the *x*-axis for every possible score cut-point. If we connect each of these intercept points with a line, it will produce an arc-shaped curve, called the *Receiver Operating Characteristics curve* (ROC curve). Don't be put off by the complicated name. It is actually just a simple graph that provides a visual representation of a screening measure's accuracy (see examples in Figures 3.1, 3.2, and 3.3). The statistic for measuring screening accuracy is the *area under the ROC curve* (or AUC). The AUC statistic is expressed as either a proportion or a percentage. A screening measure that predicts no better than chance will have an AUC value in the vicinity of 0.5 (i.e. 50% of the area on the graph falls below the ROC curve), while a 'perfect' screening instrument has an AUC of 1.0 (because the ROC curve encompasses 100% of the area on the graph). This sounds a bit esoteric, but if you look at some practical examples it starts to make sense. Below are some examples of *perfect*, *poor*, and *good* screening procedures, based on a fictional screening measure.

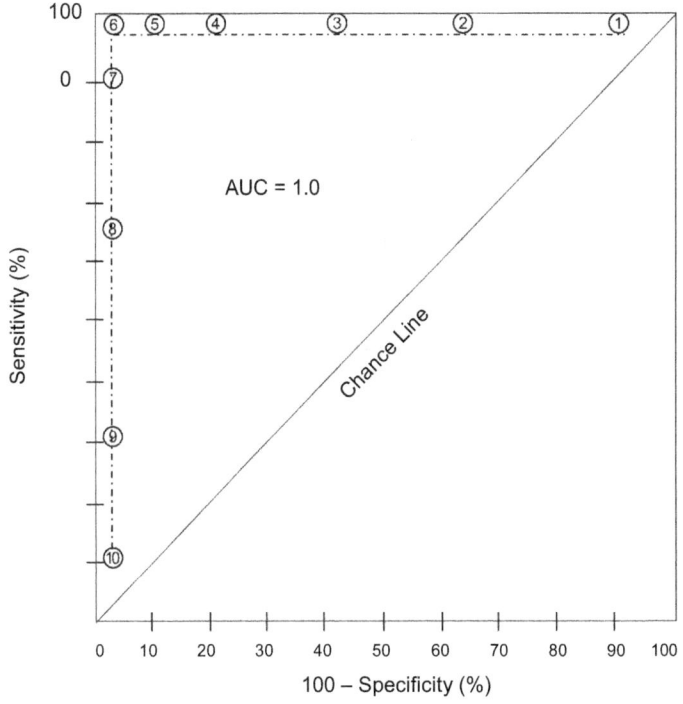

Figure 3.1 ROC curve for *perfect* screening procedure (AUC = 1.0)

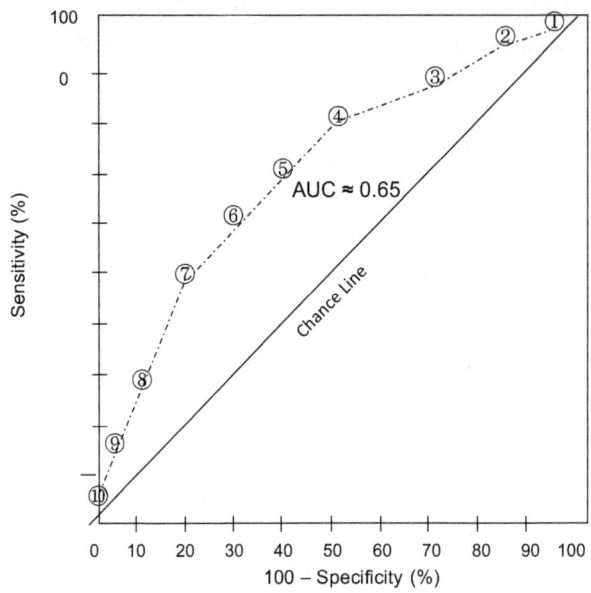

Figure 3.2 ROC curve for *poor* screening procedure (AUC ≈ 0.65)

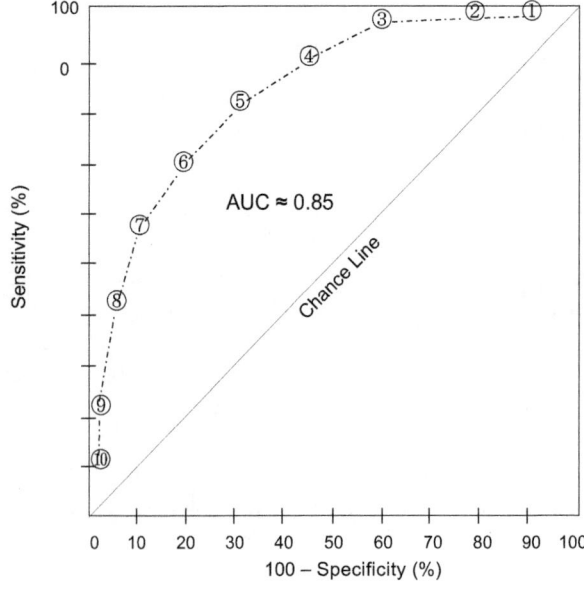

Figure 3.3 ROC curve for *good* screening procedure (AUC ≈ 0.85)

A perfect screening procedure (AUC = 1.0)

A *perfect* screening procedure correctly identifies all of the cases (i.e. children who have clinical-level difficulties) *and* all of the non-cases (children who don't have clinical-level difficulties). Table 3.1 shows an example of a perfect screening procedure. In this scenario, a fictional parent-report screening checklist yields scores ranging from zero to 10. The estimated proportions of cases and non-cases who receive each score are listed in the respective 'Score distributions' columns (4% of cases score *10*, 12% of cases score *9*, 12% of cases score *8*, etc.; while 0% of non-cases score *10*, 5% score *9*, etc.). Looking at these columns, we can see that all of the cases scored above 5, while all of the non-cases score below 6. Therefore, 100% screening accuracy can be achieved by defining scores above 5 as positive screens. This is referred to as a *6+ cut-point* (where 6+ refers to scores of 6 or higher). In this scenario, all of the cases are positive screens (100% sensitivity), and all of the non-cases are negative screens (100% specificity); there are no false identifications (no false positives, no false negatives). Figure 3.1 plots the ROC curve for this procedure, where we can see that 100% of the

Table 3.1 Example of a *perfect* screening procedure

Checklist score	Score distributions		Sensitivity	Specificity
	Cases	Non-cases		
10	10%	0%	10%	100%
9	20%	0%	30%	100%
8	35%	0%	65%	100%
7	25%	0%	90%	100%
6	10%	0%	100%	100%
5	0%	10%	100%	90%
4	0%	10%	100%	80%
3	0%	20%	100%	60%
2	0%	20%	100%	40%
1	0%	30%	100%	10%
0	0%	10%	100%	0%

area is under the curve – hence the *area under the curve* is 1.0! In practice, no screening procedure is this accurate. Instead, highly accurate tests that approach 100% accuracy are described as diagnostic tests rather than screening tests.

A poor screening procedure (AUC ≈ 0.65)

At the other extreme, a screening procedure that has an AUC around 0.65 or lower is not doing much better than chance. Such a procedure is only marginally more accurate than tossing a coin at identifying which children are cases and which are non-cases. Table 3.2 shows a different set of score distributions for cases and non-cases on our fictional screening test – which indicates this is a *poor* screening test. No score cut-point achieves an acceptable trade-off between sensitivity and specificity. The best that can be achieved is 70% sensitivity and 60% specificity at a 5+ cut-point, and 60% sensitivity and 70% specificity at a 6+ cut-point. Figure 3.2 plots the ROC curve for this procedure, which lies close to the chance line.

Table 3.2 Example of a *poor* screening procedure

Checklist score	Score distributions		Sensitivity	Specificity
	Cases	Non-cases		
10	4%	0%	4%	100%
9	12%	5%	16%	95%
8	12%	7%	28%	88%
7	20%	8%	48%	80%
6	12%	10%	60%	70%
5	10%	10%	70%	60%
4	10%	12%	80%	48%
3	8%	20%	88%	28%
2	7%	12%	95%	16%
1	5%	12%	100%	4%
0	0%	4%	100%	0%

In practice, any screening procedure that is this inaccurate should never be used.

A good screening procedure (AUC ≈ 0.85)

A screening procedure that has an AUC of 0.85 or higher will generally offer a range of screening cut-points with acceptable trade-off between sensitivity and specificity. Table 3.3 shows a third set of score distributions for cases and non-cases on our fictional screening test, which this time demonstrates good screening accuracy. The test yields two or three useful cut-points depending on the screening strategy. For a classic two-stage screening and assessment strategy, in which the first stage aims for higher sensitivity (i.e. so as to not lose too many cases in the first sweep), we might select the 4+ cut-point. If, however, the aim is to achieve a roughly even trade-off between false positives and false negatives, then we might select a 5+ cut-point. Figure 3.3 plots the ROC curve for this procedure, which lies well above the chance line.

Table 3.3 Example of a *good* screening procedure

Checklist score	Score distributions		Sensitivity	Specificity
	Cases	Non-cases		
10	10%	0%	10%	100%
9	12%	0%	22%	100%
8	20%	4%	42%	96%
7	15%	6%	57%	90%
6	12%	9%	69%	81%
5	12%	12%	81%	69%
4	9%	12%	90%	57%
3	6%	15%	96%	42%
2	4%	20%	100%	22%
1	0%	12%	100%	10%
0	0%	10%	100%	0%

Some points to consider when designing a screening strategy

Unless an instrument has a score cut-point that is 100% accurate (i.e. incurs no false positive or false negative results), then every cut-point involves a trade-off between *sensitivity* and *specificity*. Selecting optimal cut-points therefore requires subjective judgement about the relative benefits gained and costs incurred by trading sensitivity against specificity. Both the prevalence and seriousness of a health problem guide the overall screening strategy. Inaccurate screening has two main adverse implications. First, where screening fails to detect a health problem (*false negative* screens), we need to consider the implications of failing to treat this health problem. Chapter 2 details these implications as they pertain to the mental health of children in alternative care. Second, where screening incorrectly flags that someone has a health problem which they don't actually have (*false positive* screens), we need to consider the implications that this has on the person's well-being, as well as the costs of subsequent clinical assessment. Imagine, for example, the psychological distress caused by a false positive screen for cancer, or the distress to parents of a child who has a false positive screen for autism or any other serious developmental condition.

Generally, the rarer a health problem is, the more we need to focus on minimizing the false positive rate – while the more common a health problem is, the more concerned we are for minimizing the false negative rate. Let's consider for a moment that a screening procedure for detecting autism among young children has a 10% false negative rate and a 10% false positive rate. If we conservatively assume that the population prevalence of autism is 2%, then the *number* of autism cases among every 1,000 children will be 20. So among every 1,000 children screened, 2/20 children with autism (i.e. 10%) will be negative screens, and 98/980 children that do not have autism (i.e. 10%) will be positive screens. So almost all of the incorrect screens are children who don't have autism. If we instead apply the same rates to a screening procedure for detecting mental health problems among children in alternative care, where the prevalence rate of such problems is close to 50%, then the absolute number of children who are false negative screens will be much the same as the absolute number of children who are false positive screens.

Two-stage or multi-stage screening – the classic approach to screening

In most instances, the goal of mental health screening is simply to find as many children as possible who are experiencing clinically meaningful mental health difficulties, using a relatively brief and non-intrusive assessment procedure. In this context, screening is only effective when it correctly identifies the vast majority of clinical cases; conversely, it is counter-productive and harmful when it fails to detect sizeable proportions of clinical cases.

The *classic approach to screening* is to employ it as the first stage of a two-stage or multi-stage assessment strategy. The aim of the first (i.e. screening) stage is to locate as many cases as possible. The aim of the second and subsequent assessment stages is to rule out as many non-cases as possible. Therefore, when screening is the first stage of a two- or multi-stage assessment process, sensitivity is more important than specificity (except where there are seriously adverse social or emotional consequences for false positive screening, e.g. for a life-threatening illness). There are several reasons why this is particularly true for children in alternative care. First, the implications for children growing in care with undetected mental health problems are more serious than they are for children who don't have clinical-level problems being subjected to a second-stage assessment. Second, while false positive screens are likely to be correctly identified as non-cases during their second-stage assessment, there is no such remedy for false negative screens: they stay undetected. Finally, because children in care have such high prevalence of clinical level mental health difficulties (above 50%), loss of specificity within this population translates as fewer false positive screens and higher positive predictive value (the proportion of positive screens who are true cases) than occurs with mental health screening of children and young people in the general community.

Mental health monitoring by children's agencies

Mental health monitoring refers to repeated mental health measurement, which is usually planned and carried out at defined intervals, and which usually is brief in comparison to full mental health assessments. Mental health monitoring in clinical settings also typically proceeds after a larger, more comprehensive assessment. Whereas a full clinical assessment is designed to comprehensively identify a child's mental health and other pertinent psychosocial characteristics, as well as the developmental context and determinants of those characteristics, mental health monitoring is more focussed on detecting change and trajectories over time. In clinical settings the purpose of measuring changes in children's mental health over time is done for two reasons: to measure the effectiveness of psychological treatment and to determine whether a child has continuing need for a service.

What about children's agencies, particularly those that have oversight of children in statutory care? Should they also monitor children's mental health, and if so, how might such monitoring serve these children's best interests? Before I attempt to answer these questions, we need to reiterate the special duty of care that children's agencies have for children in alternative care, and especially for those children who are in statutory care. The responsibilities that children's agencies have for children in statutory care go well beyond the normal responsibilities that the state or state-sponsored agencies bear when serving the citizenry. Children's agencies hold *parental responsibility* for the children in their statutory care, even though day-to-day care and parenting is provided by individual foster parents and families. If we think for a moment of all the things that worry and concern us about our own children's well-being and futures, then imagine whose job it is to exercise the same degree of concern for children in statutory care. They certainly deserve to have as much concern invested in their well-being and futures as do our own children. In many respects there is greater need for society to be concerned about these children's well-being than that of other children. In practice, however, it has proven difficult to operationalize a level and quality of parental responsibility within children's agencies equating to what is typically exercised by parents for their own children (here I am referring to normative parental care and responsibility, not that exercised by families who maltreat their children). This is one of the main arguments for shifting children where possible from statutory care to permanent orders, such as special guardianship or adoption (Tarren-Sweeney, 2016).

So I think the answer to the question "Should children's agencies also monitor children's mental health?" is a resounding yes. First, as outlined in Chapter 2, identifying those children in care who have need for therapeutic interventions (as well as their caregivers) is profoundly important for their well-being development, and as such this is a step towards restoring their human rights. Second, a child in care's mental health provides a window to their happiness, their connectedness, their well-being, and their future lives. Third, and perhaps most importantly, if children's agencies do not monitor this very high risk population's mental health and well-being, then who does?

If we accept that children's agencies have a special responsibility for monitoring their children's mental health, then we should next consider how mental health monitoring can best serve these children's interests. Chapter 5 provides a mental health monitoring protocol that children's agencies can implement. Mental health monitoring by children's agencies serves two main purposes, both of which reflect the agencies' duty of care:

1 First, it serves the purpose of *routine mental health screening* at specified intervals. Children's mental health often changes over time, sometimes reflecting gradual alterations to children's developmental trajectories (such as those who show therapeutic recovery in response to consistent, loving care), and sometimes as a reaction to recent changes or events. Whereas a child may have screened negative for mental health difficulties in previous years, their mental health may deteriorate over a relatively short period. Unless an agency periodically screens children's mental health, they are reliant on the child's caregivers to report their concerns. Some caregivers can be reticent to report that a child in their care has deteriorating mental health (often times the first indication that this has occurred is when a placement breaks down).

2 Second, mental health monitoring helps to inform agencies about the levels of support *they* (as distinct from clinical services) should be providing to children and their caregivers, as well as planning for potential contingencies. For example, in some jurisdictions not all children in statutory care have an identified caseworker. Only children with the highest support needs have their own caseworker. While this is reprehensible, nevertheless mental health monitoring can help ensure that children with the highest support needs have a caseworker.

There are some other purposes for which mental health monitoring is employed by children's agencies, which I think are counter-productive. First, I think that linking foster-parent-reported scores on brief mental health measures to such things as fostering payments and allowances, particularly if a low score leads to the loss of money or material supports, is futile. Chapter 5 provides an overview of various contexts that can generate systematic responder bias (i.e. unreliable reporting) on screening and monitoring measures – the loss of payments or material support is definitely one of them.

Second, I think it is unhelpful and unhealthy to see children's recovery from developmentally based mental ill health as a *performance indicator* for children's agencies or post-adoption services, or for government authorities that license these agencies. While we know that children growing up in care have varied long-term mental health trajectories (some stay much the same, some deteriorate, and some improve), we don't yet have a good understanding of what accounts for this. We certainly don't have a good enough understanding of this subject to be able to tie changes in children's mental health directly to the qualities of individual placements. I refer readers to Chapter 1 for a detailed description of what accounts for the mental health difficulties of children in alternative care, and the extent to which their mental health changes while growing up in care.

References

Goodman, R. (2001). Psychometric properties of the Strengths and Difficulties Questionnaire. *Journal of the American Academy of Child & Adolescent Psychiatry*, *40*, 1337–1345.

Tarren-Sweeney, M. (2016). The developmental case for adopting children from care. *Clinical Child Psychology & Psychiatry*, *21*(4), 497–505.

4 An overview of brief caregiver-report screening and monitoring measures

In this chapter I describe and review brief caregiver-report mental health screening and/or monitoring measures that can be used by children's agencies and post-adoption services. The measures were selected for review according to the following criteria:

1 The measures are designed to be completed by parents or other primary caregivers (note that some of these measures have parallel teacher-report and/or youth self-report forms).
2 The measures are brief (defined as 50 checklist items or fewer) and are typically completed by children's caregivers in 10 minutes or less.
3 The measures are designed for mental health *screening* and/ or *brief monitoring*.
4 The measures either screen for or monitor a range of *general mental health difficulties*, or a range of *attachment- and trauma-related difficulties* as commonly experienced among children in alternative care.

This overview excludes measures that have a narrow symptomatic focus. The reason for this is that children's agencies need a relatively simple procedure that can screen for a broad range of symptomatology using one or two brief measures.

Based on these criteria, nine measures are covered in this chapter. These are summarized in Table 4.1. They include some measures that require clinical oversight by a mental health professional on staff, and some that can be administered and interpreted by agencies without professional oversight.

Table 4.1 Brief (<50 items), carer-report and youth-report mental health *screening* and/or *monitoring* measures reviewed in this chapter

Measure	Purpose		Parent-report form			Self-report form	Research with children in alternative care	Cost in 2018	Restricted to use by clinical professionals
	Screening	Monitoring	Early childhood	Middle childhood	Adolescence				
Ages and Stages Questionnaire, Social and Emotional (ASQ:SE)	✓	✗	✓ 2–60 months	✗	✗	✗	✓	US$275	✗
Assessment Checklist for Children – Short Form (ACC-SF)	✗	✓	✗	✓ 4–11	✗	✗	✓	Free	✓
Assessment Checklist for Adolescents – Short Form (ACA-SF)	✗	✓	✗	✗	✓ 12–17	✗	✓	Free	✓
BASC-3 Behavioural and Emotional Screening System (BAC3-BESS)	✓	✗	✓ 3–5	✓ 6–17	✓ 6–17	✓ 8–17	✗	US$300-$400 plus annual subscription	✓

Measure								
Brief Assessment Checklists (BAC-C, BAC-A)	✓	✓	✗	✓ 4–11	✓ 12–17	✗	✓	Free	✗
Brief Infant-Toddler Social and Emotional Assessment (BITSEA)	✓	✗	✓ 12–36 months	✗	✗	✗	✓	US$49 per every 50 administrations	✗
Brief Problem Monitor (BPM)	✗	✓	✗	✓ 6–18	✓ 6–18	✓ 12–18	✓	US$25 per every 50 administrations	✓
Pediatric Symptom Checklist 17 (PSC-17)	✓	✗	✗	✓ 4–17	✓ 4–17	✓ 11–17	✓	Free	✗
Strengths and Difficulties Questionnaire (SDQ)	✓	✓	✓ 3–4	✓ 4–17	✓ 4–17	✓ 11–17	✓	Free	✗

✓ Measure meets the criterion.
✗ Measure doesn't meet the criterion.

Ages and Stages Questionnaires:
Social-Emotional, 2nd edition (ASQ:SE-2)

Purpose:	*Screening* for broad-range mental health difficulties among infants and young children
Age range:	1 month to 6 years
Informants:	Parents and other primary caregivers
Length:	≈ 30 items per questionnaire
User qualifications:	Not explicitly stated, but publications refer to use by early child professionals. Can be purchased from the publisher without evidence of clinical registration.
Cost:	US$275 (2018)
Where to obtain:	www.brookespublishing.com/

Brief description

The *Ages and Stages Questionnaire: Social and Emotional, 2nd edition* (ASQ:SE-2) is designed to screen for difficulties across seven areas of social-emotional functioning and development in early childhood: self-regulation, compliance, adaptive functioning, autonomy, affect, social-communication, and interaction with people (Squires, Bricker, & Twombly, 2015). It consists of nine age-specific questionnaires for use at 2, 6, 12, 18, 24, 30, 36, 48, and 60 months of age.

Screening accuracy and utility

Several studies have estimated the mental health screening accuracy of the ASQ:SE for use with young children at large, such as in routine health checks in primary care settings i.e. akin to universal population screening. The screening accuracy of the ASQ:SE for different age groups were estimated within a large normative study (Squires, Bricker, Heo, & Twombly, 2001; Yovanoff & Squires, 2006). The study employed two reference standards for developmental difficulties. A social-emotional score derived from the Vineland Adaptive Behaviour Scales was the reference standard for children younger than 24 months; the CBCL clinical range was the reference standard for children aged 24 months and older.

Two divergent sets of sensitivity and specificity rates have been published for the recommended cut-off scores: one set favouring sensitivity and the other specificity (Squires et al., 2001; Yovanoff & Squires, 2006). Neither publication lists the ROC AUC statistics, making it difficult to compare its screening accuracy to that of other measures.

A recent Dutch study examined the screening accuracy of both the ASQ:SE and BITSEA at ages 6 months, 14 months, and 24 months, among a large sample of infants attending routine 'well child' paediatric checks (de Wolff, Theunissen, Vogels, & Reijneveld, 2013). The reference criterion for mental health problems was having a CBCL total problems score in the clinical range. ASQ:SE, BITSEA and CBCL scores were gathered simultaneously for 24-month-olds. However, the ASQ:SE and BITSEA scores for 6-month-olds were referenced against CBCL scores reported 12 months later (when the children were 18 months old), and the ASQ:SE and BITSEA scores for 14-month-olds were referenced against CBCL scores reported 10 months later (when the children were 24 months old). While the 24-month assessments provide a reasonable estimation of screening accuracy, we have less assurance that the relationships between ASQ:SE scores reported at ages 6 months and 14 months and CBCL scores reported a considerable time later provide a fair estimation of the ASQ:SE's screening accuracy at those ages. Instead these relationships are estimations of *predictive validity*. Looking solely at the 24-month-old sample, the AUC for ASQ:SE scores predicting CBCL clinical range scores was 0.88, and the sensitivity and specificity of the selected cut-point were 0.66 and 0.91, respectively. This compares with an AUC for 24-month BITSEA scores of 0.95, and sensitivity and specificity of 0.84 and 0.91, respectively. This provides the best direct comparison of the ASQ:SE and BITSEA, with the latter demonstrating higher screening accuracy.

A recent English study measured the accuracy of statutory health assessments, and the ASQ:SE in screening for mental disorders among 43 preschool children in foster care (Hillen & Gafson, 2014). The reference standard for identifying cases was a multidimensional clinical assessment, which identified 60% of the preschoolers as having one or more mental disorders. Against this standard, both the ASQ:SE and statutory health assessments demonstrated 35%

sensitivity, meaning they each failed to identify 65% of children who had one or more mental disorders. The ROC analysis of ASQ:SE scores yielded an unacceptably low AUC of 0.65.

Given that the prevalence of clinical-level mental health problems among young children at large is relatively low (fewer than 10%), effective mental health screening in primary care settings requires high specificity. For children at large, then, a false positive rate of 10% translates as a far greater number of children than a 10% false negative rate! In this context, cut-off scores would typically be selected to ensure at least 90% specificity. Given the much higher prevalence of mental disorders among children in alternative care, cut-off scores are ideally selected on the basis of maximizing sensitivity, rather than specificity. For this reason, the optimal ASQ:SE cut-point for use with children in alternative care is likely to be lower than the cut-point recommended by its publishers.

Conclusion

While the ASQ:SE is commonly used as a mental health screening measure for preschool children residing in alternative care, the Hillen and Gafson study results suggest it is not sufficiently accurate for use with this population, and that it greatly under-detects children who require mental health services. While one remedy may be to lower the ASQ:SE cut-point with a view to increasing the measure's sensitivity, the low AUC statistic indicates that this would require a hefty trade-off in specificity. Until further validation research is carried out on the ASQ:SE's use with children in alternative care, I would caution against employing the ASQ:SE as a screening measure with this population. Furthermore, some studies suggest the BITSEA provides more accurate mental health screening than the ASQ:SE among toddlers and preschoolers at large.

Assessment Checklist for Children – Short Form (ACC-SF)

Purpose: *Monitoring* a range of attachment- and trauma-related mental health difficulties experienced by school-aged children in alternative care that are not adequately measured by other broad-range mental health measures. The measure is derived from the long-form Assessment Checklist for Children (ACC).

Age range: Ages 4–11 years

Informants: Foster parents, adoptive parents, and other primary caregivers

Length: 44 items

User qualifications: Professional training in child mental health assessment and formulation. Users register with the measures' developer. See further details of user qualifications in the following description.

Cost: Nil

Where to obtain: www.childpsych.org.uk

Description

The *Assessment Checklist for Children Short Form* – ACC-SF is a 44-item short-form version of the 120-item *Assessment Checklist for Children* (ACC). The ACC-SF was developed primarily for use as a research instrument and as a relatively brief treatment monitoring measure. The ACC in turn was developed systematically, with a view to measuring all clinically significant problems experienced by children in alternate care that are not adequately measured by standard parent-report checklists (Tarren-Sweeney, 2014).

The ACC-SF has nine clinical scales that were empirically derived via factor analysis, and which correspond to 9 of the 10 ACC clinical scales:

   I   Sexual behaviour
  II   Pseudomature interpersonal behaviour
 III   Non-reciprocal interpersonal behaviour

   IV   Indiscriminate interpersonal behaviour
   V   Insecure interpersonal behaviour
   VI   Anxious-distrustful
   VII Abnormal pain response
   VIII Food maintenance behaviour
   IX   Self-injury.

Scale I measures age-inappropriate sexual behaviour. Scales II to
V measure various forms of maladaptive interpersonal relatedness
which are suggestive of attachment disorder behaviours and/or
attachment-related social difficulties. Scale II describes a pattern of
precious pseudomaturity and role reversal. Scale III describes emotionally withdrawn, avoidant, and non-reciprocal social behaviours,
with high scores being suggestive of a severely avoidant-insecure
attachment style and/or inhibited form of reactive attachment disorder. Scale IV describes a pattern of indiscriminate overfriendliness,
affection-seeking, and attention-seeking behaviours, resembling the
disinhibited form of reactive attachment disorder. Scale V measures
a range of social behaviours and emotional difficulties suggestive of
felt insecurity that is likely to reflect both trait insecurity (insecure
attachment, temperament) and state insecurity (e.g. as a response
to severe stressors, such as impermanent care). Scale VI measures a
pattern of trauma-related anxiety and distrust. Scale VII measures
a pattern of abnormal responses to physical hurt suggestive of pain
insensitivity or failure to communicate felt pain. Scale VIII measures
a pattern of excessive eating and food acquisition (termed *food maintenance syndrome*), that appears to be primarily triggered by acute
stress, and which resembles the behavioural correlates of hyperphagic short stature. Scale IX measures self-injurious behaviours.

   The ACC-SF scoring profile sheet is reproduced in this book in
Appendix 1. The ACC-SF record sheet is not included in this book
because it is only distributed to registered users.

Development and validation of the ACC-SF

Validity of the source measure

The ACC-SF was derived from the *Assessment Checklist for Children*
(ACC). The ACC is a 120-item caregiver-report psychiatric rating instrument measuring behaviours, emotional states, traits, and

manners of relating to others, as manifested by children in care and similar child populations (Tarren-Sweeney, 2007). The ACC's content was developed systematically, with a view to measuring all clinically significant problems experienced by children in alternate care that are not adequately measured by standard parent-report checklists. Ten clinical and two low self-esteem scales were empirically derived via factor analysis. Initial data indicate that the instrument has good content, construct, and criterion-related validity. Comprehensive survey estimates of the mental health of children in care can be obtained using the ACC in parallel with the CBCL. The instrument also provides a means for studying the characteristics and determinants of complex psychopathology manifested by child welfare populations.

Development and validity of the ACC-SF

The first step in developing a short-form version of the ACC was to limit the scope of what it measures by excluding the ACC items measuring low self-esteem, suicide discourse, the pica index, and all additional items not contributing to a clinical scale. This left a pool of 83 items that were candidates for the short-form version. A principal components factor analysis was then performed on these 83 items using 8-, 9-, and 10-factor rotations. Items that loaded strongest on the various factors were then retained for a smaller pool with a view to retaining between 4 and 6 items per short-form scale. A final 44-item analysis produced a stable 9-factor model, closely replicating the factor structure of the long-form ACC. The model accounted for 57% of the score variance. This exceeds that of most published checklists for children, as well as that of the ACC long-form 10-factor model (49%). The reason such a large proportion of the variance is accounted for by this short-form model is that it only contains the highest-loading items from the long-form version.

The internal reliability of the short-form total score (44 items) was alpha = 0.92 ($n = 347$), while the internal reliability of the six short-form scales ranged from 0.67 to 0.84. The structure and psychometric properties of the nine short-form clinical scales (factor loadings, item-rest correlations, item prevalence, and internal reliability) are listed in Table 4.2, while the ACC-SF inter-scale correlations are listed in Table 4.3.

Table 4.2 ACC-SF scales with constituent items

	Loading[a]	Item-rest[b]	Prevalence (%)[c]
I. Sexual Behaviour *(5 items, Cronbach's alpha = 0.84)*			
35 describes or imitates sexual behaviour	.71	.69	12
37 forces or pressures children into sexual acts	.82	.68	7
40 sexual behaviour not appropriate for age	.72	.70	14
42 touches or puts mouth on other person's sex parts	.65	.48	4
43 tries to involve others in sexual behaviour	.87	.77	9
II. Pseudomature *(6 items, Cronbach's alpha = 0.78)*			
21 precocious (talks, behaves like an adult)	.86	.65	32
22 prefers to be with adults, rather than children	.73	.60	32
23 prefers to mix with older children	.63	.53	40
28 too independent	.63	.48	27
29 treats you as though you were the child, and he/she was the parent	.65	.49	26
III. Non-reciprocal *(6 items, Cronbach's alpha = 0.78)*			
2 avoids eye contact	.57	.48	38
7 does not share with friends	.49	.46	40
8 does not show affection	.78	.50	23
18 lacks guilt or empathy	.62	.59	39
20 manipulates or uses friends	.50	.53	29
30 uncaring (shows little concern for others)	.71	.64	31
IV. Indiscriminate *(5 items, Cronbach's alpha = 0.78)*			
1 attention-seeking behaviour	.40	.49	74
3 changes friends quickly	.57	.49	36
15 hugs men (other than relatives or male carer)	.65	.49	20
24 relates to strangers "as if they were family"	.79	.70	47
27 too friendly with strangers	.76	.62	68

		Loading[a]	Item-rest[b]	Prevalence (%)[c]
V. Insecure *(5 items, Cronbach's alpha = 0.72)*				
4	clingy	.50	.44	52
12	fears you will reject him/her	.78	.60	31
16	is convinced that friends will reject him/her	.51	.46	20
25	seems insecure	.62	.54	44
32	worries something bad will happen to you	.71	.40	38
VI. Anxious-Distrustful *(6 items, Cronbach's alpha = 0.76)*				
5	distrusts adults	.44	.56	27
10	fearful of men in general	.63	.50	11
11	fearful or nervous at bedtime	.50	.47	13
17	is fearful of being harmed	.68	.52	17
31	wary or vigilant	.48	.51	19
38	has panic attacks	.69	.44	8
VII. Abnormal Pain Response *(4 items, Cronbach's alpha = 0.70)*				
6	does not cry	.49	.44	24
19	laughs when injured or hurt	.48	.38	16
36	does not show pain if physically hurt	.82	.69	15
44	won't say when physically hurt	.78	.48	14
VIII. Food Maintenance *(4 items, Cronbach's alpha = 0.81)*				
9	eats too much	.76	.63	25
13	gorges food	.73	.68	23
14	hides or stores food	.80	.58	14
26	steals food	.76	.61	18
IX. Self-Injury *(4 items, Cronbach's alpha = 0.67)*				
33	bites him/herself	.81	.55	9
34	causes injury to him/herself	.73	.55	10
39	hits head, head-banging	.48	.37	10
41	threatens to injure him/herself	.70	.46	3

a Factor loading.

b Item-rest correlation (correlation of the item score and the sum of all other items in the scale).

c Item prevalence (percentage of sample with item score of 1 or 2, $n = 347$).

Table 4.3 Correlations of ACC-SF (*n* = 412) scales

ACC-SF scales	Total Short Form	Sexual behaviour	Pseudomature	Non-reciprocal	Indiscriminate	Insecure	Anxious –distrustful	Abnormal pain response	Food maintenance
Sexual behaviour	.57								
Pseudomature	.68	.32							
Non-reciprocal	.76	.41	.42						
Indiscriminate	.73	.40	.41	.50					
Insecure	.70	.32	.41	.39	.42				
Anxious-distrustful	.64	.28	.43	.39	.25	.52			
Abnormal pain response	.53	.24	.34	.37	.28	.26	.23		
Food maintenance	.61	.20	.27	.40	.38	.33	.37	.27	
Self-injury	.45	.16	.15	.28	.29	.28	.27	.26	.34

Defining ACC-SF clinical and elevated ranges

Total clinical score

Clinical and elevated ranges for the ACC-SF total score were identified using a similar procedure to that used to determine clinical ranges for the ACC total score. Relationships between ACC-SF total score distributions and categorical measures of clinical status were examined for the CICS baseline cohort (*n* = 347), with a view to identifying clinically significant scores. The clinical indicators were CBCL total problems scores in the clinical range, CBCL total problems scores in the borderline plus clinical ranges, and any CBCL sub-scale score in the clinical range. Sensitivity and specificity were plotted for each criterion in Receiver Operating Characteristics (ROC) analyses. Optimal cut-points for each analysis were identified by balancing two objectives: (1) that the cut-point maximizes the number of children correctly identified and (2) that the cut-point has roughly equal sensitivity and specificity. The results of these analyses suggest there are no substantive gender differences in clinically significant scores, meaning the same clinical cut-points can be applied to both genders. Two cut-points were selected to identify children with clinically significant mental health problems. First, ACC-SF total scores of 14 and above constitute a clinical range that is highly predictive of psychiatric impairment. Second, ACC-SF scores in the range of 10–13 constitute a sub-clinical elevated range, indicating a moderate likelihood of psychiatric impairment. Although neither cut-point incurred an unreasonable compromise between specificity and sensitivity, the clinical range is highly specific (resulting in few false positives), and the elevated range is highly sensitive (few false negatives). For example, for predicting CBCL total problems scores in the clinical range, the sensitivity and specificity of the ACC-SF clinical cut-point (score = 14) were 81% and 93%, respectively, while the sensitivity and specificity of the elevated cut-point (score = 10) were 92% and 76%, respectively.

Sub-scale scores

Elevated and clinical ranges for the ACC-SF sub-scales were selected so as to attain maximum concordance with the equivalent ACC sub-scale elevated and clinical ranges. This was done by plotting the sensitivity and specificity of children's ACC-SF sub-scale scores for predicting elevated and clinical score ranges on the respective long-form scales.

Who can use the ACC-SF and ACA-SF measures?

There is a danger that ACC-SF and ACA-SF scores are inappropriately interpreted or misused by non-clinicians. These measures thus should not be employed as monitoring measures by agencies without direct oversight by qualified clinicians. It is important to emphasize that the developer does not agree to these measures being used primarily for administrative purposes by children's or health agencies.

Use of the ACC-SF and ACA-SF is restricted to:

1 Researchers and research teams carrying out relevant research;
2 Appropriately qualified child and adolescent mental health professionals and supervised trainees, such as those having

qualifications in (or being trained in) child and adolescent psychiatry, clinical psychology, child psychotherapy, and clinical child social work;

3   Developmental, educational, and/or paediatric psychologists.

The ACC-SF and ACA-SF are distributed freely to registered individuals or to a nominated person within a registered clinical or developmental/educational agency, within the terms of a limited licence agreement. Approved individuals and agencies agree to comply with user restrictions set out in the licence agreement, and not to pass the measures on to non-approved users.

These restrictions are primarily designed to stop the measures being used for non-clinical/psychosocial-developmental purposes (e.g. as an administrative tool), and to reduce the risk of children and young people being harmed or disadvantaged due to incorrect clinical formulation and labelling of their difficulties.

Conclusion

The ACC-SF provides a relatively brief measure of a range of attachment- and trauma-related mental health difficulties experienced among children placed into alternative care following chronic and severe maltreatment. While it yields less comprehensive estimates of these difficulties than the longer ACC (from which it was derived), the ACC-SF is useful for ongoing monitoring of such difficulties once a comprehensive assessment is completed, particularly when used in conjunction with a brief broad-range mental health monitoring measure, such as the SDQ. The main potential drawback for agencies is that the ACC-SF can only be used by licenced clinicians.

Assessment Checklist for Adolescents – Short Form (ACA-SF)

Purpose:	*Monitoring* a range of attachment- and trauma-related mental health difficulties experienced by young people in alternative care that are not adequately measured by other broad-range mental health measures. The measure is derived from the long-form Assessment Checklist for Adolescents (ACA).
Age range:	Ages 12–17 years
Informants:	Foster parents, adoptive parents, and other primary caregivers
Length:	37 items
User qualifications:	Professional training in child mental health assessment and formulation. Users register with the measures' developer. See further details of user qualifications in the following description.
Cost:	Nil
Where to obtain:	www.childpsych.org.uk

Description

The *Assessment Checklist for Adolescents Short Form* (ACA-SF) is a 37-item short-form version of the 105-item *Assessment Checklist for Adolescents* (ACA). The ACA-SF was developed primarily for use as a research instrument and as a relatively brief treatment monitoring measure. The ACA in turn was developed systematically, with a view to measuring all clinically significant problems experienced by adolescents in alternate care that are not adequately measured by standard parent-report checklists (Tarren-Sweeney, 2014).

The ACA-SF has six clinical scales that were empirically derived via factor analysis, and which correspond to six of the seven ACA clinical scales:

I   Non-reciprocal interpersonal behaviour
II Social instability/behavioural dysregulation

III   Emotional dysregulation/distorted social cognition
IV   Dissociation/trauma symptoms
 V   Food maintenance behaviour
VI   Sexual behaviour.

Scale I describes emotionally withdrawn, avoidant and non-reciprocal social behaviours, with high scores being suggestive of a severely avoidant-insecure attachment style and/or inhibited form of reactive attachment disorder. Scale II describes a complex combination of unstable, attachment-related social relatedness difficulties, and behavioural dysregulation (the corresponding ACA scale incorporates the majority of items contained in the ACC Pseudomature and Indiscriminate scales). Scale III describes a pattern of highly dysregulated emotion and affective instability, coupled with distorted social cognition (negative attributions, paranoid beliefs). Scale IV measures a pattern of trauma-related dissociation and anxiety symptoms. Scale V measures a pattern of excessive eating and food acquisition (termed *food maintenance syndrome*), that appears to be primarily triggered by acute stress, and which resembles the behavioural correlates of hyperphagic short stature. Scale VI measures age-inappropriate sexual behaviour.

The ACA-SF scoring profile sheet is reproduced in this book in Appendix 2. The ACA-SF record sheet is not included in this book because it is only distributed to registered users.

Development and validation of the ACA-SF

Validity of the source measure

The ACA-SF was derived from the *Assessment Checklist for Adolescents* (ACA). The ACA is a 105-item, caregiver-report, psychiatric rating scale that measures behaviours, emotional states, traits, and manners of relating to others as manifested among 12- to 17-year-old young people in care, as well as young people who are adopted from care or who have a history of maltreatment (Tarren-Sweeney, 2013a). The ACA was designed to measure a broad range of mental health difficulties observed among young people in various types of care, that are not adequately measured by standard rating instruments, such as the CBCL, SDQ, and Conners scales. The ACA has seven clinical scales and two low self-esteem scales that were empirically derived through factor analysis. Initial data indicate that the instrument has good content, construct, and criterion-related validity. Comprehensive survey estimates of the mental health of adolescents in care can be obtained using the ACA in parallel with the CBCL. The instrument also provides a means for studying the characteristics and determinants of complex psychopathology manifested by child welfare populations.

Development and validity of the ACA-SF

The first step in developing a short-form version of the ACA was to limit the scope of what it measures by excluding the ACA items measuring low self-esteem, suicide discourse, and all additional items not contributing to a clinical scale. This left a pool of 66 items that were candidates for the short-form version. A principal components factor analysis was then performed on these 66 items using 5-, 6-, and 7-factor rotations. Items that loaded strongest on the various factors were then retained for a smaller pool with a view to retaining between 5 and 8 items per short-form scale. A final 37-item analysis produced a stable 6-factor model, closely replicating the factor structure of the long-form ACA. The short-form 'social instability' factor has a stronger emphasis on attachment-related social difficulties, and less emphasis on behavioural dysregulation, than the equivalent long-form factor, and hence the label for the short-term scale does not refer to behavioural dysregulation. The model accounted for 57% of the score variance. This exceeds that of most published checklists for children, as well as that of the ACA long-form 7-factor model (51%). The reason such a large proportion of the variance is accounted for by this short-form model is that it only contains the highest-loading items from the long-form version.

The internal reliability of the short-form total score (37 items) was alpha = 0.91 (n = 230), while the internal reliability of the six short-form scales ranged from 0.73 to 0.87. The structure and psychometric properties of the six short-form clinical scales (factor loadings, item-rest correlations, item prevalence, and internal reliability) are listed in Table 4.4, while the ACA-SF inter-scale correlations are listed in Table 4.5.

Table 4.4 ACA-SF scales with constituent items

		Loading[a]	Item-rest[b]	Prevalence (%)[c]
I. Non-reciprocal *(6 items, Cronbach's alpha = 0.79)*				
2	does not show affection	.81	.58	31
6	hides feelings	.69	.57	47
12	refuses to talk	.60	.45	20
14	resists being comforted when hurt	.70	.54	26
16	seems alone in the world (not connected to people or places)	.61	.54	25
21	withdrawn	.73	.56	23
II. Social instability *(8 items, Cronbach's alpha = 0.84)*				
1	craves affection	.50	.54	38
8	impulsive (acts rashly, without thinking)	.51	.58	57
9	precocious (talks or behaves like an adult)	.82	.60	29
10	prefers to be with adults, rather than peers	.88	.62	25
11	prefers to mix with older youths	.78	.54	33
13	relates to strangers as if they were family	.52	.62	26
19	too friendly with strangers	.62	.58	42
20	tries too hard to please other young people	.53	.55	33
III. Emotional dysregulation/distorted social cognition *(7 items, Cronbach's alpha = 0.82)*				
15	says friends are against him/her	.60	.55	23
17	startles easily ('jumpy')	.49	.48	17
23	can't get scary thoughts or images out of his/her head (not due to watching a scary movie)	.76	.54	10
25	extreme reaction to losing a friend, or being excluded	.75	.62	11
32	intense reaction to criticism	.57	.60	34
33	says his/her life is not worth living	.79	.64	9
37	uncontrollable rage	.57	.65	23

		Loading[a]	Item-rest[b]	Prevalence (%)[c]
IV. Dissociation/trauma symptoms *(6 items, Cronbach's alpha = 0.73)*				
22	appears dazed, 'spaced out' (like in a trance)	.49	.49	20
24	can't tell if an experience is real or a dream	.62	.58	10
26	feels like things, people or events aren't real	.53	.59	4
28	has panic attacks	.60	.46	11
29	has periods of amnesia (e.g. has no memory of what has happened in the last hour)	.52	.51	10
30	hits head, head-banging	.60	.39	7
V. Food maintenance *(5 items, Cronbach's alpha = 0.87)*				
3	eats secretly (e.g. in the middle of the night)	.84	.73	20
4	eats too much	.77	.72	30
5	gorges food	.64	.67	23
7	hides or stores food	.83	.65	13
18	steals food	.85	.73	15
VI. Sexual behaviour *(5 items, Cronbach's alpha = 0.84)*				
27	forces or pressures other youth or children into sexual acts	.79	.67	3
31	inappropriately shows genitals to others (in person, or through video or photo)	.76	.62	3
34	seems overly preoccupied with sex (e.g. crude sexual talk, inappropriate sexual comments)	.68	.61	9
35	sexual behaviour not appropriate for age	.75	.70	7
36	tries to involve others in sexual behaviour	.92	.75	3

a Factor loading.

b Item-rest correlation (correlation of the item score and the sum of all other items in the scale).

c Item prevalence = percentage of the CICS sample ($n = 230$) with item score of 1 or 2.

Table 4.5 Correlations of ACA-SF (*n* = 230) scales

ACA-SF scales	Total Short Form	Non-reciprocal	social instability	Emotional dysregulation/ distorted Social Cognition	Dissociation/trauma sym.	Food maintenance
Non-reciprocal	.61					
Social instability	.80	.33				
Emotional dysregulation/ distorted social cognition	.74	.35	.47			
Dissociation/trauma sym.	.67	.30	.32	.55		
Food maintenance	.69	.30	.44	.37	.44	
Sexual behaviour	.57	.18	.43	.28	.42	.36

Defining ACA-SF clinical and elevated ranges

Total clinical score

Clinical and elevated ranges for the ACA-SF total score were identified using a similar procedure to that used to determine clinical ranges for the ACA total score. Relationships between ACA-SF total score distributions and categorical measures of clinical status were examined for the CICS follow-up and adolescent survey samples (*n* = 230), with a view to identifying clinically significant scores. The clinical indicators were CBCL total problems scores in the clinical range, CBCL total problems scores in the borderline plus clinical ranges, and any CBCL sub-scale score in the clinical range. Sensitivity and specificity were plotted for each criterion in Receiver Operating Characteristics (ROC) analyses. Optimal cut-points for each analysis were identified by balancing two objectives: (1) that the cut-point maximizes the number of young people correctly identified; and (2) that the cut-point has roughly equal sensitivity and specificity. The results of these analyses suggest there are no substantive gender differences in clinically significant scores, meaning the same clinical cut-points can be applied to both genders. Two cut-points were selected to identify young people with clinically significant mental health problems. First, ACA-SF total scores of 12 and above constitute a clinical range that is highly predictive of psychiatric impairment. Second, ACA-SF scores in the range of 9–11 constitute a sub-clinical elevated range, indicating a moderate likelihood of psychiatric impairment. Although neither cut-point incurred an unreasonable compromise between specificity and sensitivity, the clinical range is highly specific (resulting in few false positives), and the elevated plus clinical range is highly sensitive (few false negatives). For example, for predicting CBCL total problems scores in the clinical range, the sensitivity and specificity of the ACA-SF clinical cut-point (score = 12) were 82% and 92%, respectively, while the sensitivity and specificity of the elevated cut-point (score = 8) were 93% and 76%, respectively.

Clinical sub-scale scores

Elevated and clinical ranges for the ACA-SF sub-scales were selected so as to attain maximum concordance with the equivalent ACA sub-scale elevated and clinical ranges. This was done by plotting the sensitivity and specificity of children's ACA-SF sub-scale scores for predicting elevated and clinical score ranges on the respective long-form scales.

Who can use the ACC-SF and ACA-SF measures?

There is a danger that ACC-SF and ACA-SF scores are inappropriately interpreted or misused by non-clinicians. These measures thus should not be employed as monitoring measures by agencies without direct oversight by qualified clinicians. It is important to emphasize that the developer does not agree to these measures being used primarily for administrative purposes by children's or health agencies.

Use of the ACC-SF and ACA-SF is restricted to:

1   Researchers and research teams carrying out relevant research;
2   Appropriately qualified child and adolescent mental health professionals and supervised trainees, such as those having

qualifications in (or being trained in) child and adolescent psychiatry, clinical psychology, child psychotherapy, and clinical child social work;

3   Developmental, educational, and/or paediatric psychologists.

The ACC-SF and ACA-SF are distributed freely to registered individuals or to a nominated person within a registered clinical or developmental/educational agency, within the terms of a limited licence agreement. Approved individuals and agencies agree to comply with user restrictions set out in the licence agreement, and not to pass the measures on to non-approved users.

These restrictions are primarily designed to stop the measures being used for non-clinical/psychosocial-developmental purposes (e.g. as an administrative tool), and to reduce the risk of children and young people being harmed or disadvantaged due to incorrect clinical formulation and labelling of their difficulties.

Conclusion

The ACA-SF provides a relatively brief measure of a range of attachment- and trauma-related mental health difficulties experienced among children placed into alternative care following chronic and severe maltreatment. While it yields less comprehensive estimates of these difficulties than the longer ACA (from which it was derived), the ACA-SF is particularly useful for ongoing monitoring of such difficulties once a comprehensive assessment is completed, particularly when used in conjunction with a brief broad-range mental health monitoring measure, such as the SDQ. The main potential drawback for agencies is that the ACA-SF can only be used by licenced clinicians.

BASC-3 Behavioral and Emotional Screening System (BASC3-BESS)

Purpose:	*Screening* for broad-range mental health difficulties
Age range:	Ages 3–17 years
Informants:	Parents and other primary caregivers, teachers, child self-report (8 years and older)
Length:	29 items
User qualifications:	Qualification Level B (Pearson). Training in child mental health assessment.
Cost:	US$300–$400 (2018) initial cost plus annual subscription
Where to obtain:	www.pearsonclinical.com

Brief description

The *BASC-3 Behavioral and Emotional Screening System* (BASC3-BESS; Kamphaus & Reynolds, 2015) and *BASC-2 Behavioral and Emotional Screening System* (BASC2-BESS; Kamphaus & Reynolds, 2007) are short-form versions of the BASC-2 and BASC-3 that are ostensibly designed for use as screening measures. I refer to both editions of this measure as they are both being marketed by the publisher (as of January 2018), and the screening accuracy of the newer version has yet to be investigated.

The BASC3-BESS Parent form is a 29-item general mental health measure that yields a single total problems score for preschool-aged children through to Year 12 adolescents. The BESS also has teacher-report and self-report (from Grade 3) versions. While various screening data have been reported for the teacher-report and child self-report versions, there do not yet appear to be any research estimates of the mental health screening accuracy of the parent-report form for either the second or third edition. One study calculated moderate correlations between BASC2-BESS parent-report scores and parent-reported scores on the CBCL DSM-oriented scales, suggesting this measure has good potential for mental health screening (Dowdy, Kamphaus, Abdou, & Twyford, 2013). As yet, however, no estimates of the screening accuracy (as measured by ROC analysis, or sensitivity and specificity rates) of either the BASC2-BESS or BASC3-BESS parent-report form have been reported. Agencies should not consider using the parent-report versions of the measures for mental health screening until their screening accuracy has been confidently established.

Brief Assessment Checklists (BAC-C and BAC-A)

Purpose:	*Screening* for and *monitoring* a range of attachment- and trauma-related mental health difficulties experienced by children and young people in alternative care, that are not adequately measured by broad-range mental health measures. The measures are derived from the long-form *Assessment Checklist for Children* (ACC) and *Assessment Checklist for Adolescents* (ACA)
Age ranges:	BAC-C, 4–11 years; BAC-A, 12–17 years
Informants:	Foster parents, adoptive parents, and other primary caregivers
User qualifications:	No restrictions on who can score and interpret these measures
Cost:	Nil
Where to obtain:	www.childpsych.org.uk

Brief description

The *Brief Assessment Checklist for Children* (BAC-C) and the *Brief Assessment Checklist for Adolescents* (BAC-A) are 20-item caregiver-report psychiatric rating scales designed to:

1 Screen for clinically meaningful mental health difficulties experienced by children and adolescents in various types of care;
2 Be used as brief casework monitoring tools by alternative care and post-adoption support agencies, and for treatment monitoring in CAMHS;
3 Be safely administered and interpreted by health and social care professionals other than child and adolescent mental health clinicians.

The BAC-C and BAC-A were derived from the *Assessment Checklist for Children* (ACC, 120 items) and *Assessment Checklist for Adolescents* (ACA, 105 items), respectively. The BAC-C and BAC-A record forms are listed at the back of this book as Appendices 3 and 4, respectively.

Rationale for developing the Brief Assessment Checklists

Available mental health screening instruments for school-aged children and adolescents are designed to screen for the symptoms and disorders most commonly encountered among the population at large, particularly anxiety, depression, peer socialization difficulties, inattention/overactivity, aggression and other conduct problems, and oppositional-defiant behaviour. Prior to the development of the BAC, no instrument had been designed to screen for additional characteristic difficulties experienced by children and young people in care that the ACC and ACA were designed to measure, notably *various trauma- and attachment-related* difficulties. Just as there is a need for clinicians to have tools that contribute to their comprehensive assessment of these difficulties, there is also an evident need for tools that accurately screen for these difficulties.

There are two reasons why the ACC and ACA are not suitable for use as screening and casework monitoring measures. First, they have too many items (120 and 105, respectively) to qualify as brief, easy-to-complete measures. Second, given the nature of some of the problems measured by these checklists and the labels given to their empirically derived scales, it is the developer's belief that the ACC and ACA cannot be safely used by people other than qualified child and adolescent mental health professionals. Without adequate training in clinical and psychosocial-developmental formulation, users are likely to misinterpret the meaning of high scale scores, and children are more likely to be labelled as having particular attachment- and/or trauma-related difficulties, based on a single source of information. Consequently, use of the ACC and ACA is restricted to qualified clinicians and researchers. Yet, child welfare and social care agencies have a legitimate need to carry out mental health screening and monitoring for vulnerable children and young people in their statutory care, particularly in jurisdictions that do not have a proactive primary care mental health service for children in care. Furthermore, primary health care workers who are responsible for carrying out health screening may not have adequate training in mental health assessment to interpret the meaning of ACC and ACA score profiles.

Together this constitutes a rationale for developing brief screening versions of the ACC and ACA that (1) have high screening accuracy; (2) provide a single total difficulties score, that is without any constituent sub-scales; and (3) can be safely used and interpreted by social care and health professionals other than child mental health clinicians.

Validity and reliability of the Brief Assessment Checklists for use as brief monitoring measures

Population distributions of BAC scores

Population distributions of BAC-C and BAC-A scores have to date been estimated in two representative studies: the CICS surveys in which the measures were developed, and a recent population survey of Dutch children in foster care (Goemans, Tarren-Sweeney, van Geel, & Vedder, 2017).

In the CICS, mean (standard deviation) BAC-C total difficulties scores for the aggregate 4- to 11-year-old sample ($N = 347$), boys ($N = 176$), and girls ($N = 171$) were 10.0 (8.0), 9.9 (7.6), and 10.2 (8.4), respectively, suggesting the score distributions did not vary by gender. Mean (standard deviation) BAC-A total difficulties scores for the aggregate 11- to 18-year-old sample ($N = 230$), boys ($N = 125$), and girls ($N = 105$) were 8.5 (7.6), 9.0 (7.7), and 7.8 (7.4), respectively, suggesting a slight gender variation in the adolescent score distributions. Consistent with previously reported age analyses of ACC (Tarren-Sweeney, 2007) and ACA scores (Tarren-Sweeney, 2013a), older pre-adolescent children scored slightly higher on the BAC-C than younger children (age − total score correlation = 0.16), with this age effect being confounded by children's age at entry into care (older children were more likely to have entered care at older ages, and with greater exposure to pre-care maltreatment), whereas no age effect was located among BAC-A scores (age − total score correlation = −0.02).

The levels of BAC difficulties reported for Dutch foster children were notably higher than that reported for the NSW children. Mean (standard deviation) BAC-C and BAC-A scores for Dutch children and adolescents were 12.1 (8.2) and 11.5 (7.8), respectively. This is despite the fact that mean Dutch SDQ scores were closely comparable to mean NSW SDQ-proxy (see description of the SDQ-proxy scores derived from the CBCL in Chapter 5) scores. Together these results suggest that the Dutch samples had higher BAC scores relative to their general mental health difficulties than did the NSW samples – in other words, it suggests that their symptomatology profiles are skewed towards relatively higher attachment- and trauma-related difficulties.

Validity

In the CICS, very high correlations were found between BAC-C and ACC total scores ($r = 0.96$) and BAC-A and ACA total scores ($r = 0.94$). Similarly high correlations were found between BPM scores (generated from sample CBCL scores) and CBCL scores for the child ($r = 0.93$) and adolescent ($r = 0.94$) samples. Correlations of BAC-C and BAC-A total scores with the CBCL total problem score were 0.82 and 0.88, respectively. By contrast, a weighted mean correlation of parent-report SDQ total difficulties scores with CBCL total problems scores for 4- to 12-year-olds, estimated across several studies, was 0.76 (range $= 0.70$–0.87) (Stone, Otten, Engels, Vermulst, & Janssens, 2010), while the correlation of parent-report BESS scores with CBCL total problems scores in a recent survey of primary-school children ($n = 99$) was 0.63 (Dowdy et al., 2013).

The present findings suggest the BAC-C/A total scores approximate the CBCL total problem score (a measure of global psychopathology) at least as well as the SDQ total difficulties score, but not as well as the BPM (which is derived from the CBCL, and is reviewed later in this chapter). Correlations of BAC-C and BAC-A scores with the SDQ total difficulties score in the Dutch survey were 0.83 and 0.80, respectively (Goemans et al., 2017). Two recent online surveys of the mental health of English children ($N = 190$; Frogley, 2016) and adolescents ($N = 111$; Denton, 2016) residing in family-based statutory care included the BAC and SDQ. Average BAC and SDQ scores in both surveys were very high, possibly reflecting participant selection bias (the studies recruited 'convenience' samples via foster parent organizations). Correlations of BAC-C and BAC-A scores with the SDQ total difficulties score in these English surveys were 0.72 and 0.75, respectively. Together these results suggest the BAC-C/A total difficulties scores provide comparable estimations of global psychopathology to those suggested by SDQ, CBCL, ACC, and ACA total scores.

Correlations of BAC-C and BAC-A total scores measured in the CICS with relevant ACC and ACA clinical scales and with CBCL syndrome, DSM-oriented and BPM scales are listed in Table 4.6. BAC-C/A total scores had moderate to high correlation (0.67–0.88) with the ACC and ACA scales that measure commonly

Table 4.6 Correlations of BAC-C and BAC-A total scores with ACC, ACA, and CBCL scale scores

	BAC-C	BAC-A		BAC-C	BAC-A
ACC and ACA scales			**CBCL scales**		
Total clinical	.96	.94	Total problems	.82	.88
Sexual behaviour	.63	.46	Anxious/depressed	.61	.65
Non-reciprocal	.79	.73	Withdrawn/depressed	.57	.61
Food maintenance	.51	.55	Somatic complaints	.41	.38
Suicide discourse	.32	.27	Social problems	.71	.75
Low self-esteem	.75	.68	Thought problems	.73	.71
ACC-only scales			Attention problems	.66	.69
Pseudomature	.76		Rule-breaking behaviour	.70	.72
Indiscriminate	.79		Aggressive behaviour	.69	.83
Insecure	.82				
Anxious-distrustful	.67		DSM affective problems	.62	.58
Abnormal pain response	.53		DSM anxiety problems	.58	.61
Self-injury	.44		DSM somatic problems	.34	.29

(Continued)

Table 4.6 (Continued)

	BAC-C	BAC-A		BAC-C	BAC-A
ACA-only scales			DSM attention deficit/hyp.	.64	.72
Social-behavioural dysregulation		.88	DSM oppositional defiant	.61	.71
Dissociation/trauma symptoms		.51	DSM conduct problems	.63	.78
Dysregulated emotion/distorted social cognition		.80	Brief Problem Monitor (BPM)	.74	.83

experienced difficulties, and moderate correlation (0.27–0.63) with scales measuring lower prevalence difficulties. There were mostly moderate to high correlations of BAC-C/A total scores with CBCL syndrome and DSM-oriented scale scores. The notable exceptions were quite low correlations with the two CBCL somatic scales. This is largely accounted for by a relatively low prevalence (compared to other symptoms) of reported somatic problems among children and adolescents in the CICS, and low correlations of CBCL somatic complaints/problems scores with other CBCL scale scores (Tarren-Sweeney & Hazell, 2006). In the Dutch survey, there were moderate to high correlations between BAC-C/BAC-A scores and SDQ sub-scale scale scores. Correlations between BAC-C scores and the SDQ internalizing problems, externalizing problems and prosocial behaviour scores were 0.76, 0.67, and −0.44, respectively; while correlations between BAC-A scores and these SDQ sub-scales were 0.69, 0.65, and −0.52, respectively (Goemans et al., 2017).

Internal consistency

The internal consistency (Cronbach's alpha) of BAC-C and BAC-A scores in the CICS, Dutch, the aforementioned English surveys (Denton, 2016; Frogley, 2016), and a survey of clinic-referred

English children adopted from care (King, Gieve, Iacopini, Hahne, & Stradling, 2017; Tarren-Sweeney et al., in press), as well as the internal consistency of child and adolescent SDQ scores in the Dutch and English surveys, are listed in Table 4.7. These studies consistently indicate that the BAC-C and BAC-A have good internal reliability, slightly exceeding that of the SDQ.

The internal consistency of the derived parent–report BPM total score in the CICS child and adolescent samples was 0.88 (17 items) and 0.91 (19 items), respectively, which is similar to that previously reported for a large U.S. normative sample ($N = 3,200$, $\alpha = 0.92$; Achenbach, McConaughy, Iyanova, & Rescorla, 2011). BAC-C/A internal consistencies are thus somewhat comparable to that of the parent-report BPM, while they compare favourably to a large number of published estimates of the internal consistency of the SDQ parent-report total difficulties scale (weighted mean SDQ total difficulties alpha = 0.80, range = 0.53–0.84; Stone et al., 2010).

Table 4.7 Internal consistency (Cronbach's alpha) of BAC and SDQ total difficulties scores

	Child (4–11)			*Adolescent (12–17)*		
	N	*BAC-C*	*SDQ*	*N*	*BAC-A*	*SDQ*
Survey						
Australia (CICS, foster care) (Tarren-Sweeney, 2007, 2013b)	*347*	$\alpha = .89$	N/A	*230*	$\alpha = .87$	N/A
Netherlands (foster care) (Goemans et al., 2017)	*118*	$\alpha = .89$	$\alpha = .85$	*101*	$\alpha = .84$	$\alpha = .84$
England (foster care) (Denton, 2016; Frogley, 2016)	*190*	$\alpha = .89$	$\alpha = .67$	*111*	$\alpha = .89$	$\alpha = .85$
England (adoption) (Tarren-Sweeney et al., in press)	*473*	$\alpha = .84$	$\alpha = .82$	*244*	$\alpha = .78$	$\alpha = .73$

Screening accuracy of the Brief Assessment Checklists

The accuracy with which the BAC correctly identified dichotomous indicators of clinical symptomatology, mental health service use, and caregiver stress in the NSW (Tarren-Sweeney, 2013b) and Dutch (Goemans et al., 2017) studies is listed in Table 4.8. The table lists the AUC statistics generated from ROC analyses (see Chapter 3 for an explanation of AUC and ROC analyses). In the CICS, both the BAC-C and BAC-A were *highly accurate* in screening for clinical and 'elevated or clinical' range ACC and ACA scores, with AUCs ranging from 0.96 to 0.99. They were

Table 4.8 Screening accuracy of the BAC-C and BAC-A in the CICS and Dutch studies

Study	*Case criterion*	*BAC-C, Ages 4–11*		*BAC-A, Ages 12–17*	
		Case prevalence	*AUC (95% CI)*	*Case prevalence*	*AUC (95% CI)*
Dutch	Intervention[a]	51%	.72 (.63, .81)	42.6%	.76 (.66, .86)
	High carer Stress	41%	.79 (.71, .88)	40%	.87 (.80, .95)
NSW	Diagnosis or intervention[b]	69%	.75 (.70, .81)	67%	.78 (.71, .84)
	ACC/ACA clinical score[c]	45%	.99 (.98, 1.00)	37%	.99 (.98, 1.00)
	CBCL clinical score[d]	46%	.92 (.89, .95)	38%	.94 (.91, .97)
	ACC/ACA or CBCL clinical score[e]	52%	.96 (.94, .98)	43%	.97 (.95, .99)

a Child and/or foster parent receiving therapeutic intervention or behavioural support.
b Foster-parent-reported diagnosis, or receiving intervention (including foster parent intervention), or seeking intervention.
c ACC (child) or ACA (adolescent) total clinical score in clinical range.
d CBCL total problem score in clinical range.
e ACC (child) or ACA (adolescent) total clinical score and/or CBCL total problem score, in clinical range.

also *moderately accurate* in screening for CBCL clinical and 'borderline or clinical' range scores, with AUCs ranging from 0.89 to 0.92 for the BAC-C and 0.93 to 0.94 for the BAC-A. Their screening accuracy for identifying CBCL total scores in the clinical range (AUC = 0.92 and 0.94) compares favourably with the accuracy of parent-report SDQ total difficulties scores in predicting clinical range CBCL total scores (AUC = 0.85), in a health screening study of 7- to 12-year-old Dutch children (N = 711; Mathilde R. Crone, personal communication, 1 November 2012; Crone, Vogels, Hoekstra, Treffers, & Reijneveld, 2008).

In both the NSW (CICS) and Dutch studies, the BAC-C and BAC-A were moderately accurate in screening for children's present treatment status, with AUCs ranging from 0.72 to 0.78 (see Table 4.8). We would not expect accuracy to be much higher than this, given that many children in care that have clinical-level difficulties are not receiving clinical interventions. The BAC-C and BAC-A were also moderately accurate in screening for high foster parent stress in the Dutch survey.

Optimal screening cut-points for children in primary care

The method for identifying the optimal BAC-C and BAC-A screening cut-points and information about how to use these measures are covered in Chapter 5.

Brief Infant-Toddler Social and Emotional Assessment (BITSEA)

Purpose:	*Screening* for broad-range mental health difficulties among toddlers. The BITSEA is derived from the long-form Infant-Toddler Social and Emotional Assessment (ITSEA).
Age range:	Ages 1–3 years
Informants:	Parents and other primary caregivers
Length:	42 items
User qualifications:	Qualification Level B (Pearson), Allied Health or Education professional. Agencies can purchase if they have registered social workers, nurses or similar professions overseeing the screening.
Cost:	US$49 (2018) per bundle of 50 report forms
Where to obtain:	www.pearsonclinical.com.au/products/view/56

Brief description

The *Brief Infant-Toddler Social and Emotional Assessment* (BITSEA) is a brief (42-item) measure of social-emotional/behavioural problems and competence among 12- to 36-month-old children. It includes a 31-item problem index that measures internalizing, externalizing, and dysregulation difficulties. Two screening cut-points are applied to the problem index score. The first cut-point defines a clinical range, encompassing 15% of the normative sample, and the second cut-point defines an 'of concern' range, encompassing 25% of the normative sample (Briggs-Gowan, Carter, Irwin, Wachtel, & Cicchetti, 2004).

Screening accuracy

Three studies have estimated the mental health screening accuracy of the BITSEA among community and primary care samples (Briggs-Gowan et al., 2004; de Wolff et al., 2013; Kruizinga,

Jansen, Mieloo, Carter, & Raat, 2013), and a fourth study included sub-samples of clinic-referred and community non-referred children (Briggs-Gowan et al., 2013).

The screening accuracy of the BITSEA problem index score was examined in the measure's initial validation study (N = 1,237, age range 12–25 months; Briggs-Gowan et al., 2004). The clinical reference standards included 'clinical range' and 'borderline or clinical range' scores on the CBCL. Different cut-points were selected for each combination of gender and 6-month age ranges. The sensitivity and specificity rates (combined across all age ranges and both genders) for these various cut-points were 93% and 78%, respectively, for detecting CBCL clinical range scores, and 81% and 83%, respectively, for detecting CBCL 'clinical *or* borderline' range scores.

A study of 213 clinic-referred (N = 103) and non-referred (N = 110) 2- and 3-year-olds residing with a custodial parent (i.e. excludes children in foster care) estimated the BITSEA's screening accuracy against two clinical reference criteria: scores in the CBCL clinical range and diagnoses derived from a semi-structured psychiatric interview (Briggs-Gowan et al., 2013). Overall screening accuracies as estimated by the AUC statistic were not published. However, very good sensitivity and specificity rates were reported for both the 'clinical' and 'of concern' cut-points, using both clinical reference standards. In predicting psychiatric disorders, sensitivity and specificity rates for the 'clinical' cut-point were 73% and 82%, respectively, and using the 'of concern' cut-point were 79% and 71%, respectively. In predicting 'any CBCL clinical range score', sensitivity and specificity rates for the 'clinical' cut-point were 84% and 89%, respectively, and using the 'of concern' cut-point were 93% and 79%, respectively (Briggs-Gowan et al., 2013).

A recent Dutch study examined the screening accuracy of the BITSEA problem index score in a community sample of 2,060 2-year-olds (Kruizinga et al., 2013). Once again, the clinical reference standard was CBCL total problem scores in the clinical range. In this study the BITSEA problem index score was extremely accurate in predicting CBCL clinical range scores, with an AUC of 0.97 and the optimal cut-point yielding 95% sensitivity and 90% specificity.

Another recent Dutch study examined the screening accuracy of both the BITSEA and ASQ:SE at ages 6 months, 14 months, and 24 months, among a large sample of infants attending routine 'well child' paediatric checks (de Wolff et al., 2013). The reference criterion for mental health problems was having a CBCL total problems score in the clinical range. BITSEA, ASQ:SE, and CBCL scores were gathered simultaneously for 24-month-olds. However, the ASQ:SE and BITSEA scores for 6-month-olds were referenced against CBCL scores reported 12 months later (when the children were 18 months old), and the ASQ:SE and BITSEA scores for 14-month-olds were referenced against CBCL scores reported 10 months later (when the children were 24 months old). While the 24-month assessments provide a reasonable estimation of screening accuracy, we have less assurance that the relationships between BITSEA scores reported at ages 6 months and 14 months and CBCL scores reported a considerable time later provide a fair estimation of the BITSEA's screening accuracy at those ages. Instead these relationships are estimations of *predictive validity*. Looking solely at the 24-month-old sample, the AUC for BITSEA scores predicting CBCL clinical range scores was 0.95, and the sensitivity and specificity of the selected cut-point were 0.84 and 0.91, respectively. This compares with an AUC for 24-month ASQ:SE scores of 0.88, and sensitivity and specificity of 0.66 and 0.91, respectively. This provides the best direct comparison of the BITSEA and ASQ:SE in this age range, with the former demonstrating higher screening accuracy for 2-year-olds in the general community.

Conclusion

Among children at large, the BITSEA problem index score provides accurate screening for mental health difficulties of 12- to 36-month-old toddlers, insofar as the CBCL total problems clinical range provides a reliable indication of clinical-level mental health difficulties. Furthermore, one direct comparison of the BITSEA and ASQ:SE suggests the former is the more accurate mental health screener for toddlers at large. However, the BITSEA's screening accuracy has yet to be measured with toddlers residing in alternative care. The ASQ:SE's poorer screening accuracy when used with young children in foster care, in comparison to how it performs with children at large, suggests the possibility that the BITSEA could also perform less well with toddlers in alternative care.

Brief Problem Monitor (BPM)

Purpose:	*Monitoring* broad-range mental health difficulties. The BPM is derived from the long-form ASEBA scales (i.e. CBCL/TRF/YSR).
Age range:	6–18 years
Informants:	Parents and other primary caregivers, teachers and adolescent self-report (12 years and older)
Length:	Between 18 and 22 items
User qualifications:	Masters level training or professional registration relevant to child mental health assessment and formulation
Cost:	US$25 (2018) per bundle of 50 report forms
Where to obtain:	www.aseba.org

Brief description

The *Brief Problem Monitor* (BPM) is a 22-item cross-informant version of the CBCL (and its equivalent teacher- and self-report forms), that was developed recently to monitor children's functioning and response to therapeutic interventions (Achenbach et al., 2011). Nineteen of the BPM items were derived from the CBCL internalizing (6 items), externalizing (7 items), and attention problems (6 items) scales, and 3 items are respondent-nominated 'additional items'. Although it was not expressly designed for use as a screening instrument, the BPM's brevity will likely see it increasingly used for that purpose, particularly if it is shown to have comparable or better screening utility to the SDQ. However, the BPM contains no items from the Social problems and Thought problems syndrome scales, which children and young people in care score highly on.

Monitoring validity and reliability

Various validity and reliability data for the BPM have been derived and published from the US ASEBA (CBCL/TRF/YSR) normative datasets (Achenbach et al., 2011). Test-retest reliability is especially critical for monitoring measures. In the normative sample, the test-retest reliability of the BPM parent-report form scales ($N = 73$) were: $r = 0.81$ (internalizing score); $r = 0.83$ (attention problems); $r = 0.83$ (externalizing problems), and $r = 0.85$ (total problems).

The internal consistencies (Cronbach's alpha; $N = 3,210$) of these four scales were 0.80, 0.85, 0.88, and 0.92, respectively. A recent online community survey ($N = 567$) estimated very similar internal consistencies, namely 0.78 (internalizing), 0.87 (attention problems), 0.86 (externalizing), and 0.91 (total problems). Internal consistency is high relative to the small number of items in each scale (Piper, Gray, Raber, & Birkett, 2014).

In my NSW Children in Care Study, BPM scores were derived from children's CBCL scores with a view to examining the BPM's potential as a screening measure for use with children in alternative care. The internal consistency of the derived parent-report BPM total score in the CICS child ($N = 347$) and adolescent ($N = 230$) samples was 0.88 (17 items) and 0.91 (19 items), respectively, which is comparable to that reported in the community and normative studies. This is also comparable to the internal consistency of other well-designed brief measures, notably the SDQ.

As expected, in the CICS BPM scores and CBCL total problems scores correlated very highly in the child ($r = 0.93$) and adolescent ($r = 0.94$) samples. However, correlations between BPM scores and the ACC and ACA total clinical scores were also high ($r = 0.78$ and $r = 0.80$, respectively). The correlations between the BPM and BAC short-form measures were $r = 0.74$ for the child sample and $r = 0.83$ for the adolescent sample. These latter inter-scale correlations are comparable to the short-form BAC-SDQ correlations found in the Dutch population study ($r = 0.83$ and $r = 0.80$, respectively) (Goemans et al., 2017), and the BAC-Proxy-SDQ correlations found in CICS ($r = 0.76$ and $r = 0.84$, respectively).

Screening accuracy

While the BPM's developers did not propose its use as a screening measure, its screening accuracy for use with children in foster care was estimated in the CICS child and adolescent surveys. This was possible because the BPM items are contained within the CBCL, which was included in both of the CICS surveys. The accuracy of the BPM in screening for a range of clinical reference criteria in the CICS surveys is compared to the screening accuracy of the BAC,

Table 4.9 Screening accuracy (AUC) for identifying various caregiver-reported clinical indicators: comparison of BPM, BAC, ACC/ACA, and CBCL scores in the CICS surveys

	Area under the ROC curve		
	Reported mental health service use[a]	Reported diagnosis[b]	Reported medication[c]
Child sample (N = 347)			
BPM (17 items)	**0.75**	**0.78**	**0.71**
BAC-C (20 items)	0.74	0.73	0.63
ACC (102 items)	0.75	0.75	0.65
CBCL (120 items)	0.78	0.78	0.69
Adolescent sample (N = 230)			
BPM (19 items)	**0.79**	**0.78**	**0.83**
BAC-A (20 items)	0.79	0.77	0.79
ACA (87 items)	0.82	0.81	0.80
CBCL (120 items)	0.81	0.80	0.82

a Foster-parent-reported use of mental health services within last year or was actively seeking a mental health service.
b Foster parent report of child's mental health diagnosis.
c Foster parent report of psychiatric/behavioural medication.

ACC, and CBCL measures in Table 4.9. These findings suggest the BPM has comparable screening accuracy to the comparison measures, at least with respect to predicting these specific clinical criteria.

Conclusion

The Brief Problem Monitor was specifically developed to monitor changes in children's mental health during treatment. Its good test-retest reliability suggests that it is psychometrically stable over time, such that score changes over time are not accounted for by unreliable reporting. The BPM also performed well in the large CICS surveys of children and adolescents in foster care. Potential disadvantages for agencies using the BPM are that the record sheets cost $1 per administration, and its use is restricted to staff with clinical or developmental training.

Pediatric Symptom Checklist 17 (PSC-17)

Purpose:	*Screening* for broad-range mental health difficulties
Age range:	Ages 4–17 years
Informants:	Parents and other primary caregivers, adolescent self-report (11 years and older)
Length:	17 items
User qualifications:	No restrictions on who can score and interpret these measures
Cost:	Nil
Where to obtain:	www.massgeneral.org/psychiatry/services/psc_forms.aspx

Brief description

The *Pediatric Symptom Checklist 17* (PSC-17) is a brief mental health screening measure designed for use in primary care and general paediatric settings (Gardner et al., 1999). It is commonly used in North America, in contrast to Europe and Australasia where the SDQ dominates. The PSC-17 was derived in the late 1990s from the 35-item *Pediatric Symptom Checklist*, the latter also being a popular screening measure in North America. Aside from a total problem score (17 items), the PSC-17 yields internalizing (5 items), externalizing (7 items), and attention problems (5 items) sub-scale scores.

Screening accuracy

While there has been a fair amount of research into the PSC-17's standard psychometric properties (i.e. that are relevant to its use as a mental health monitoring measure), I have only managed to locate two studies that estimated the PSC-17's screening accuracy. In a large U.S. study ($N = 18,045$) of children attending primary paediatric clinics, PSC-17 scores were referenced against dichotomous mental health case assignment, based on mental health clinic records (Gardner et al., 1999). AUCs ranged from 0.83 to 0.89, and optimal cut-points yielded sensitivity rates from 0.77 to 0.87

and specificity rates from 0.68 to 0.80. Another U.S. study of children attending routine primary health clinics ($N = 269$) compared the PSC-17's screening accuracy with that of several longer measures, including the CBCL and the Child Depression Inventory (Gardner, Lucas, Kolko, & Campo, 2007). The clinical reference criterion was psychiatric diagnoses identified by a structured psychiatric interview. The AUCs for the CBCL total problems score and the PSC-17 predicting any psychiatric diagnosis were 0.78 and 0.74, respectively, which are fairly modest. No cut-point on either measure provided an acceptable trade-off between sensitivity and specificity. However, the most surprising finding was that the CBCL total problems score did not accurately predict any psychiatric diagnosis. It is possible that these results are at least partly accounted for by the case assignment methodology.

Conclusion

A recent U.S. cross-state survey of mental health screening practices by child welfare services identified the PSC-17 as being the most commonly used standardized mental health screening measure used by such services in the United States (Hayek et al., 2014). Yet, despite such widespread use, there is limited evidence of the PSC-17's screening accuracy with children at large, and to my knowledge there is no evidence of its screening accuracy with child welfare populations. This contrasts markedly with the large body of evidence supporting use of the SDQ with both community and 'in care' child populations in Europe, as well as two recent U.S. studies (Conn, Szilagyi, Alpert-Gillis, Baldwin, & Jee, 2016; Jee et al., 2011).

Strengths and Difficulties Questionnaire (SDQ)

Purpose: *Screening* for and *monitoring* broad-range mental health difficulties
Age range: Ages 3–17 years
Informants: Parents and other primary caregivers, teachers, adolescent self-report (11 years and older)
Length: 25 items
User qualifications: No restrictions on who can score and interpret these measures
Cost: Nil
Where to obtain: www.sdqinfo.com

Brief description

The *Strengths and Difficulties Questionnaire* (SDQ) is a brief assessment and screening measure of children's general mental health difficulties and prosocial behaviour (Goodman, 2001), that utilizes parent-report (ages 3–4 and 4–16), teacher-report (ages 3–4 and 4–16), and adolescent self-report (ages 11–17) forms. The SDQ has 25 items, consisting of 20 symptom items that constitute a total difficulties scale and four clinical sub-scales (emotional symptoms, conduct problems, hyperactivity-inattention, and peer problems), and 5 prosocial behaviour items. The instrument also includes questions designed to measure how a child's mental health difficulties impact on their functioning and well-being, and what burden these place on others. The developers distribute a computer algorithm that predicts psychiatric disorder by combining the SDQ problem scores and impact scores from multiple informants. This algorithm can be run in either SPSS, SAS, or STATA statistical software.

Despite its brevity, the SDQ has strong psychometric properties (particularly for the teacher version) and has demonstrated screening utility (Stone et al., 2010). It is also readily accessible in that it has no user restrictions and is distributed freely as a non-commercial instrument. For all of these reasons, the SDQ has become the most widely used and well-recognized child and adolescent screening measure in Europe and Australasia (less so in North America).

Validity and reliability of the caregiver-report form of the Strengths and Difficulties Questionnaire for use as brief monitoring measure

Population distributions of caregiver-reported SDQ scores for children in alternative care

Mean caregiver-reported SDQ total difficulties scores obtained in 13 population surveys of children and young people in alternative care, as well as rates of SDQ total difficulties scores falling within the clinical ranges, are listed in Table 4.10. This table reveals that SDQ mean total difficulties scores are remarkably consistent across the various national samples, in relation to the type of alternative care that the children are placed in. With the exception of the Norwegian study, mean SDQ total scores for representative samples of children in foster care were closely aligned, ranging from about 11 to 13; while children in residential care, 'difficult to place' foster children, and aggregate samples of children that included those in residential care had higher scores.

Validity

The SDQ's construct validity is demonstrated through evidence of good factorial, concurrent, and criterion-referenced validity. Furthermore, the accumulated research evidence confirms that the SDQ total difficulties score provides a good estimation of children's global psychopathology. Several studies have endorsed the SDQ 5-factor structure through confirmatory factor analysis (Sanne, Torsheim, Heiervang, & Stormark, 2009), including one study of foster-parent-reported SDQs (Lehmann et al., 2017). Concurrent validity is demonstrated by moderate correlations of SDQ scores with other validated, broad-range mental health measures. Parent-report SDQ total difficulties scores for ages 4–12 have an average correlation of $r = 0.76$ (range = 0.70–0.87) with CBCL total problems scores across a large number of studies (Stone et al., 2010).

With regard to children in alternative care, correlations of foster-parent-reported SDQ total difficulties scores with BAC-C and BAC-A scores in a Dutch population survey were 0.83 and 0.80, respectively (Goemans et al., 2017). Two recent online surveys of the mental health of English children ($N = 190$; Frogley, 2016)

Table 4.10 Distributions of caregiver-reported Strengths and Difficulties Questionnaire (SDQ) total difficulties scores for various populations of children in alternative care

Study	Location	Type of care	Age	N	Mean total difficulties score	Borderline or clinical range[a]	Clinical range
Goemans et al. (2017)	Netherlands	Foster	4–11	118	12.9	40%	35%
Goemans et al. (2017)	Netherlands	Foster	12–17	101	11.7	37%	28%
Maaskant, Van Rooij, and Hermanns (2014)	Netherlands	Foster	4–12	239	11.6	N/A[b]	N/A
Janssens and Deboutte (2009)	Belgium	Foster	3–17	71	12.8	N/A	30%
Lehmann, Boe, and Breivik (2017)	Norway	Foster	6–12	237	15.2	N/A	N/A
Conn et al. (2016)	U.S.	Foster	5–17	237	N/A	71% on *any* of the five sub-scales	N/A
Jee et al. (2011)	U.S.	Foster	11–17	138	N/A	N/A	30%
Staines (2012)	U.K.	Foster children, *difficult to place*	5–14	299	15.4	64%	39%

Study	Country	Care type	Age range	N	Mean SDQ		
Department for Education (2016)	U.K. (England)	Mixed (annual statutory reporting for English children in care, 74% response rate)	5–16	27,610	14.0	51%	38%
Rees (2013)	U.K.	Mixed (foster, residential, kin)	7–15	193	16.3	61%	47%
Milburn, Lynch, and Jackson (2008)	Australia	Mixed (foster, residential, kin)	4–18	161	N/A	72%[c]	N/A
Egelund and Lausten (2009)	Denmark	Mixed (foster and residential)	11	433	N/A	65%	48%
Marquis and Flynn (2009)	Canada	Mixed (foster and group homes)	11–15	492	N/A	51%	32%
Janssens and Deboutte (2009)	Belgium	Residential	3–17	138	17.1	N/A	53%

a Using U.K. published cut-points for total difficulties score (borderline cut-point = 14+, clinical cut-point = 17+).
b This study published ranges using alternative cut-points suggested for the Netherlands.
c SDQ scores gathered at entry into care, not a cross-sectional sample.

and adolescents ($N = 111$; Denton, 2016) residing in family-based statutory care included SDQ and BAC scores. Correlations of SDQ total difficulties scores with BAC-C and BAC-A scores in these English surveys were 0.72 and 0.75, respectively.

Internal consistency

The internal reliability (internal consistency, as indicated by Cronbach's alpha) of the parent-report SDQ total difficulties scale has been calculated in numerous studies. An analysis of studies reporting this statistic calculated a weighted mean alpha of 0.80 (range = 0.53–0.84; Stone et al., 2010), confirming the SDQ total score has very good internal consistency. Internal consistency of SDQ total difficulties scores in three surveys of children residing in alternative care are compared with that of BAC-C and BAC-A scores in Table 4.7. These surveys reveal varying results, with the SDQ showing greatest internal reliability in the Dutch survey (0.84, 0.85). They also suggest the BAC has slightly better internal reliability than the SDQ when used with the same study samples.

External reliability

The weighted mean test-retest correlation of parent-report total difficulties scores derived from six studies was $r = 0.76$ (range = 0.72–0.86; Stone et al., 2010), which indicates the SDQ has good test-retest reliability. The weighted mean parent-teacher inter-rater correlation for the SDQ total difficulties scores, derived from eight studies, was $r = 0.44$ (range = 0.37–0.62; Stone et al., 2010), suggesting the SDQ has modest inter-rater agreement. However, this level of parent-teacher agreement generally exceeds that found with the longer CBCL/TRF measures (Tarren-Sweeney, Hazell, & Carr, 2004). Poor inter-rater agreement, whether it be parent–teacher, parent–youth, or teacher–youth, is an intractable challenge for child psychopathology assessment. The SDQ performs as poorly in this regard as most other validated measures, but no worse than other measures.

Screening accuracy

The SDQ's accuracy in screening for clinical-level mental health difficulties among children in the general community has been investigated in several well-designed studies. ROC analyses of parent-reported total difficulties scores in eight screening studies yielded AUCs between 0.64 and 0.91 (i.e. ranging from poor to excellent), with an average weighted AUC of 0.87 (Stone et al., 2010). However, the published SDQ cut-points favour specificity over sensitivity, such that a sizeable proportion of children who have clinical-level difficulties are not identified by SDQ screening.

There is reasonable evidence that caregiver-report SDQ total difficulties scores and impact scores are moderately accurate at screening for elevated and/or clinical-level mental health difficulties among children in care. Among a sample of 223 Norwegian children in foster care, the accuracy with which the SDQ total difficulties score screened for children with one or more mental disorders (as identified by the DAWBA) was AUC = 0.83, while the screening accuracy of the impact score was AUC = 0.80 (Lehmann, Heiervang, Havik, & Havik, 2014). However, the presently endorsed cut-points have insufficient sensitivity, at least when decisions are based on a single informant. In a survey of 1,028 5- to 17-year-old English children in statutory care, the SDQ multi-informant computer algorithm (combined parent- and teacher-reported SDQ problem and impact scores) predicted the presence of a mental disorder with 85% sensitivity and 80% specificity (Goodman, Ford, Corbin, & Meltzer, 2004). Otherwise, parent- and teacher-reported SDQ scores had unacceptable sensitivity when not used in combination with the other (perhaps suggesting that the cut-points are too high), while adolescent self-report SDQs identified very few of the cases missed by the parent and teacher SDQs.

Youngest age for administering the SDQ

There is some ambiguity regarding the youngest age for administering the SDQ. The developers' website states that the SDQ is designed for 3- to 16-year-olds. However, the relevant preschool-aged parent-report record form, as well as other locations on the website refer to "2- to 4-year-olds". Looking more closely at the various national norms listed on the website, the youngest children included in national norms are 30-month-olds (2.5 years) in Glasgow, Scotland. Furthermore, the youngest children in alternative care for whom SDQ research scores have been published are 3 years old (see Table 4.9). Based on this information, I would advise against using the SDQ with 2-year-old children in alternative care, particularly given there is an acceptable alternative for that age (the BITSEA).

Optimal screening cut-points for children in alternative care

The method for identifying the optimal SDQ screening cut-points for children and adolescents, and information about how to use the SDQ, are covered in Chapter 5.

References

Achenbach, T., McConaughy, S., Iyanova, M., & Rescorla, L. (2011). *Manual for the ASEBA Brief Problem Monitor (BPM).* Burlington, VT: ASEBA.

Briggs-Gowan, M., Carter, A., Irwin, J., Wachtel, K., & Cicchetti, D. (2004). The Brief Infant-Toddler Social and Emotional Assessment: Screening for social-emotional problems and delays in competence. *Journal of Pediatric Psychology, 29,* 143–155.

Briggs-Gowan, M., Carter, A., McCarthy, K., Augustyn, M., Caronna, E., & Clark, R. (2013). Clinical validity of a brief measure of early childhood social-emotional/behavioral problems. *Journal of Pediatric Psychology, 38*(5), 577–587.

Conn, A., Szilagyi, M., Alpert-Gillis, L., Baldwin, C., & Jee, S. (2016). Mental health problems that mediate treatment utilization among children in foster care. *Journal of Child and Family Studies, 25,* 969–978.

Crone, M., Vogels, A., Hoekstra, F., Treffers, P., & Reijneveld, S. (2008). A comparison of four scoring methods based on the parent-report Strengths and Difficulties Questionnaire as used in the Dutch preventative child health care system. *BMC Public Health, 8,* 106.

Denton, R. (2016). The assessment of mental health in looked-after adolescents: An exploratory study of the Brief Assessment Checklist for Adolescents. (Doctor of Psychology), University of Surrey, Guilford, UK.

Department for Education. (2016). *Children looked after in England including adoption: 2015 to 2016.* London: Department for Education.

de Wolff, M., Theunissen, M., Vogels, A., & Reijneveld, S. (2013). Three questionnaires to detect psychosocial problems in toddlers: A comparison of the BITSEA, ASQ-SE, and KIPPPI. *Academic Pediatrics, 13,* 587–592.

Dowdy, E., Kamphaus, R., Abdou, A., & Twyford, J. (2013). Detection of symptoms of prevalent mental health disorders of childhood with the parent form of the Behavioral and Emotional Screening System. *Assessment for Effective Intervention, 38*(3), 192–198.

Egelund, T., & Lausten, M. (2009). Prevalence of mental health problems among children placed in out-of-home care in Denmark. *Child and Family Social Work, 14,* 156–165.

Frogley, C. (2016). *Assessing the mental health needs of looked after children: A study investigating the utility of the Brief Assessment Checklist for Children.* Doctor of Psychology, University of Surrey, Guilford, UK.

Gardner, W., Lucas, A., Kolko, D., & Campo, J. (2007). Comparison of the PSC-17 and alternative mental health screens in an at-risk primary care sample. *Journal of the American Academy of Child and Adolescent Psychiatry, 46,* 611–618.

Gardner, W., Murphy, J., Childs, G., Kelleher, K., Pagano, M., & Jellinek, M. (1999). The PSC-17: A brief pediatric symptom checklist with psychosocial problem subscales: A report from PROS and ASPN. *Ambulatory Child Health, 5,* 225–236.

Goemans, A., Tarren-Sweeney, M., van Geel, M., & Vedder, P. (2017). Psychosocial screening and monitoring for children in foster care: Psychometric properties of the Brief Assessment Checklists in a Dutch population study. *Clinical Child Psychology & Psychiatry,* 1–16. https://doi.org/10.1177/1359104517706527

Goodman, R. (2001). Psychometric properties of the Strengths and Difficulties Questionnaire. *Journal of the American Academy of Child & Adolescent Psychiatry, 40,* 1337–1345.

Goodman, R., Ford, T., Corbin, T., & Meltzer, H. (2004). Using the Strengths and Difficulties Questionnaire (SDQ) multi-informant algorithm to screen looked-after children for psychiatric disorders. *European Child and Adolescent Psychiatry, 13*(Suppl. 2), 25–31.

Hayek, M., Mackie, T., Mule, C., Bellonci, C., Hyde, J., Bakan, J., & Leslie, L. (2014). A multi-state study on mental health evaluation for children entering foster care. *Administration and Policy in Mental Health and Mental Health Services Research, 41,* 552–567.

Hillen, T., & Gafson, L. (2014). Statutory health assessments for pre-school foster children fail to screen accurately for mental health disorders. *Clinical Child Psychology & Psychiatry, 19*(2), 313–327.

Janssens, A., & Deboutte, D. (2009). Screening for psychopathology in child welfare: The Strengths and Difficulties Questionnaire (SDQ) compared with the Achenbach System of Empirically Based Assessment (ASEBA). *European Child and Adolescent Psychiatry, 18,* 691–700.

Jee, S., Szilagyi, M., Conn, A., Nilsen, W., Toth, S., Baldwin, C., & Szilagyi, G. (2011). Validating office-based screening for psychosocial strengths and difficulties among youths in foster care. *Pediatrics, 127*(5), 904–910.

Kamphaus, R., & Reynolds, C. (2007). *Behavior Assessment System for Children-second edition (BASC-2): Behavioral and Emotional Screening System (BESS).* Bloomington, MN: Pearson.

Kamphaus, R., & Reynolds, C. (2015). *Behavior Assessment System for Children-third edition (BASC-3): Behavioral and Emotional Screening System (BESS).* Bloomington, MN: Pearson.

King, S., Gieve, M., Iacopini, G., Hahne, A., & Stradling, H. (2017). *The evaluation of the Adoption Support Fund.* London: Department for Education.

Kruizinga, I., Jansen, W., Mieloo, C., Carter, A., & Raat, H. (2013). Screening accuracy and clinical application of the Brief Infant-Toddler Social and Emotional Assessment (BITSEA). *PLoS ONE, 8*(8), e72602.

Lehmann, S., Boe, T., & Breivik, K. (2017, June 30). The internal structure of foster-parent completed SDQ for school-aged children. *PLoS ONE,* 1–11.

Lehmann, S., Heiervang, E., Havik, T., & Havik, O. (2014). Screening foster children for mental disorders: Properties of the Strengths and Difficulties Questionnaire. *PLoS ONE, 9*(7). https://doi.org/10.1371/journal.pone.0102134

Maaskant, A. M., Van Rooij, F. B., & Hermanns, J. M. (2014). Mental health and associated risk factors of Dutch school aged foster children placed in long-term foster care. *Children & Youth Services Review, 44,* 207–216.

Marquis, R. A., & Flynn, R. J. (2009). The SDQ as a mental health measurement tool in a Canadian sample of looked-after young people. *Vulnerable Children and Youth Studies, 4,* 114–121.

Milburn, N., Lynch, M., & Jackson, J. (2008). Early identification of mental health needs for children in care: A therapeutic assessment programme for statutory clients of child protection. *Clinical Child Psychology and Psychiatry, 13*(1), 31–47.

Piper, B., Gray, H., Raber, J., & Birkett, M. (2014). Reliability and validity of Brief Problem Monitor, an abbreviated form of the Child Behavior Checklist. *Psychiatry and Clinical Neurosciences, 68*(10), 759–767.

Rees, P. (2013). The mental health, emotional literacy, cognitive ability, literacy attainment and 'resilience' of 'looked after children': A multidimensional, multiple-rater population based study. *British Journal of Clinical Psychology, 52,* 183–198.

Sanne, B., Torsheim, T., Heiervang, E., & Stormark, K. (2009). The Strengths and Difficulties Questionnaire in the Bergen Child Study: A conceptually and methodically motivated structural analysis. *Psychological Assessment, 21*(3), 352–364.

Squires, J., Bricker, D., Heo, K., & Twombly, E. (2001). Identification of social-emotional problems in young children using a parent-completed screening measure. *Early Childhood Research Quarterly, 16,* 405–419.

Squires, J., Bricker, D., & Twombly, E. (2015). *ASQ:SE-2 user's guide.* Baltimore, MD: Brookes.

Staines, J. (2012). Fostered children's behavioural and emotional difficulties: Findings from one independent foster care agency. *Clínica y Salud, 23*(3), 205–219.

Stone, L., Otten, R., Engels, R., Vermulst, A., & Janssens, J. (2010). Psychometric properties of the parent and teacher versions of the Strengths and

Difficulties Questionnaire for 4- to 12-year olds: A review. *Clinical Child and Family Psychology Review, 13,* 254–274.

Tarren-Sweeney, M. (2007). The Assessment Checklist for Children (ACC): A behavioral rating scale for children in foster, kinship and residential care. *Children & Youth Services Review, 29,* 672–691.

Tarren-Sweeney, M. (2013a). The Assessment Checklist for Adolescents (ACA): A scale for measuring the mental health of young people in foster, kinship, residential and adoptive care. *Children and Youth Services Review, 35,* 384–393.

Tarren-Sweeney, M. (2013b). The Brief Assessment Checklists (BAC-C, BAC-A): Mental health screening measures for school-aged children and adolescents in foster, kinship, residential and adoptive care. *Children and Youth Services Review, 35*(5), 771–779.

Tarren-Sweeney, M. (2014). *Clinician's guide to the Assessment Checklist series: Specialized mental health measures for children in care.* London: Routledge.

Tarren-Sweeney, M., Goemans, A., van Geel, M., Vedder, P., Hahne, A. S., & Gieve, M. (in press). Mental health screening for children in care using the Strengths and Difficulties Questionnaire and the Brief Assessment Checklists: Guidance from three national studies. *Developmental Child Welfare.*

Tarren-Sweeney, M., & Hazell, P. (2006). The mental health of children in foster and kinship care in New South Wales, Australia. *Journal of Paediatrics & Child Health, 42,* 91–99.

Tarren-Sweeney, M., Hazell, P., & Carr, V. (2004). Are foster parents reliable informants of children's behaviour problems? *Child: Care, Health and Development, 30*(2), 167–175.

Yovanoff, P., & Squires, J. (2006). Determining cutoff scores on a developmental screening measure: Use of receiver operating characteristics and item response theory. *Journal of Early Intervention, 29,* 48–62.

5 A mental health screening and monitoring protocol for children's agencies

In this chapter I propose a simple protocol for children's agencies to safely perform routine mental health screening and monitoring for the children in their charge. I work through this protocol by addressing a series of seven interconnected questions, namely:

> Q1. Which children should be only be assessed and monitored by clinicians?
> Q2. Who should complete the measures?
> Q3. What is doable for children's agencies?
> Q4. When and how often should screening and monitoring be done?
> Q5. What situations can bias caregiver's reports of children's mental health?
> Q6. Which measures should agencies use?
> Q7. What are the optimal screening cut-points for the SDQ and BAC?

Q1. Which children should only be assessed and monitored by clinicians?

I recommend that the follow groups of children only be assessed or monitored by professionals with relevant clinical and/or developmental training and experience:

1 Infants younger than 12 months old
2 Children with moderate to severe intellectual disability

3 Children who are presently receiving a clinical service, where the clinical team is carrying out comprehensive assessment or clinical monitoring
4 Children and young people residing in residential care.

Infants younger than 12 months old

To my knowledge there are no mental health screening or monitoring measures that are valid for infants under 12 months old that can be administered by untrained personnel. The BITSEA is valid from 12 to 36 months, while there isn't sufficient evidence to support the use of the ASQ:SE from 6 months of age, at least for infants in care.

Children with moderate to severe intellectual disability

There is some evidence to support the use of regular mental health measures when assessing children with *mild* and *borderline* intellectual disability, but not those with *moderate to severe* disabilities. Regarding my own Assessment Checklist series of measures (including the ACC-SF, ACA-SF, BAC-C, and BAC-A), I provide the following information in the clinical manual:

> The Assessment Checklist measures were developed and standardised using data obtained in the various stages of the NSW Children in Care study. The study samples included sizeable proportions of children having borderline to mild intellectual (around 22.4%) and other learning difficulties, comparable to that reported among other care populations, but the CICS excluded children having moderate to severe intellectual difficulties. The ACC and ACA item analyses did not reveal any validity concerns for using these instruments with children with mild intellectual disabilities or other types of learning difficulties (such as reading problems). However, these instruments are unlikely to provide valid measurement of the types of mental health difficulties manifested by children having moderate to severe intellectual disability. The Assessment Checklist measures may be used for mental health assessment

of children and young people who have a mild intellectual disability or other types of learning difficulties, but should not be used for assessment of children who have a moderate to severe intellectual disability.

(Tarren-Sweeney, 2014)

Mental health assessments of children with moderate to severe intellectual disabilities is quite specialized work, and employs standardized measures for this population, such as the Developmental Behaviour Checklist (Einfeld & Tonge, 1995). I believe that all children in care with a moderate to severe intellectual disability should undergo specialist developmental and clinical assessments.

Children who are presently receiving a clinical service, where the clinical team is carrying out comprehensive assessment or clinical monitoring

In situations where children have been assessed by a clinical service and are receiving ongoing treatment and/or monitoring from that clinical service, agencies should suspend their own routine monitoring of those children's mental health. At the very least, this will minimize the demands placed on children's foster parents or other caregivers to fill out multiple mental health measures.

Children and young people residing in residential care

Clinical professionals should be tasked with assessing and monitoring the mental health of all children and young people in residential care. Placing any child or young person into residential care is a critical event in their lives, and in western jurisdictions at least should really only occur because they could not be stably placed in family-based care. In this context, children placed into residential care in preference to family-based alternative care mostly have behavioural and/ or social relatedness difficulties, which are generally attachment-and/or trauma-related. I can think of no justification for employing mental health screening with this population – they should undergo universal comprehensive clinical/psychosocial-developmental assessment. Furthermore, routine monitoring of their mental health needs to be overseen by clinicians.

Q2. Who should complete the measures?

Adult mental health assessment is largely based on clinical interviews with the adult client, self-reported psychometric measures, and the clinician's observations of their client. The extent to which child mental health assessment is based on information directly gained from the child – whether that be from interviews, observations, or self-report measures – is somewhat age dependent. Generally speaking, the younger the child is, the more his or her assessment relies on information provided by their parents or other primary caregivers, as well as their teachers and childcare staff. Furthermore, other factors come to play in adolescence that can reduce the reliability of *some* self-reported information, even though adolescents have the cognitive capacity to reflect on and accurately report their behaviour, feelings, and thoughts.

For children and young people at large, there is a growing literature base describing the relative reliability of parent-report, teacher-report, and self-report scores on various types of mental health measures, most notably on cross-informant measures such as the Achenbach System of Empirically Based Assessment (ASEBA: CBCL/TRF/YSR) (Achenbach & Rescorla, 2001), the SDQ (Goodman, 2001), and the Conners Comprehensive Behaviour Rating Scales (Conners, 2008). Older children and adolescents in the general population *who are not referred to mental health services* (i.e. the normative population) report a higher level of mental health difficulties than that reported by their parents. But the situation is different for clinic-referred adolescents. They report less externalizing difficulties (e.g. conduct problems, disruptive behaviour, defiance) than their parents, while various studies have found that clinic-referred youth report more internalizing difficulties (e.g. anxiety and depression symptoms) than do their parents (Smith, 2007). A notable exception to this latter finding is found in the U.S. clinic-referred normative sample for the ASEBA, in which adolescents and parents reported the same level of internalizing difficulties (Achenbach & Rescorla, 2001).

Otherwise, the consensus view is that parents and teachers are more reliable informants of child and adolescent disruptive behaviours, and older children and adolescents are the most reliable informants of their internalizing symptoms.

However, there are several reasons why the research carried out on children and families at large may not apply so well to children in alternative care. First, we cannot necessarily presume that foster parents and residential care workers who have known children for relatively short periods of time will have the same depth of understanding of their children's mental health difficulties, as parents generally do. There are also specific contextual pressures within care systems that may account for foster parents or residential carers providing unreliable reports of children's difficulties (which I cover later in this chapter). Similarly, there are various contextual and psychosocial reasons why children and young people in alternative care may provide less reliable accounts of their own difficulties than do children and young people at large.

Are foster parents reliable informants of children's behaviour problems?

This is an important question for researchers and clinicians alike. Foster and adoptive parents and other alternate caregivers report high rates of psychological morbidity among children in care. In spite of this, it has been suggested that their mental health problems may be under-reported by foster parents (Halfon, Mendonca, & Berkowitz, 1995). There has also been speculation that behavioural reports by alternate caregivers can be biased by contextual issues (such as an impending placement decision; Garland, Landsverk, Hough, & Ellis-Macleod, 1996). While this need not infer that the reports of foster parents are more susceptible to bias, it is conceivable that foster parents might report the behaviour of children differently from birth parents. The experience of caring for many children with severe behavioural difficulties could influence a foster parent's rating of such behaviour. The length of time that a foster parent has known a child, as well as the strength of their relationship with that child, may also influence how they interpret the child's problem behaviour.

In the small pilot stage of my NSW Children in Care Study, I measured greater inter-rater agreement (a measure of reliability) between foster parents' and teachers' reports of children's mental health difficulties (using the CBCL and the teacher-report version of the CBCL, the TRF), than that found in comparison studies of parent-teacher agreement using the same measures (Achenbach & Edelbrock, 1986; McConaughy, Stanger, & Achenbach, 1992; Sawyer, Baghurst, & Clark, 1992; Verhulst & Akkerhuis, 1989). Furthermore, the low correlation between foster parent and teacher scores for internalizing behaviour was no better or worse than that found in comparison studies of parent–teacher agreement (Achenbach & Edelbrock, 1986; McConaughy et al., 1992; Sawyer et al., 1992; Verhulst & Akkerhuis, 1989; Verhulst & Van der Ende, 1991). The children had been with their foster parents for an average of 3 years (i.e. these were long-term placements).

The CICS results provides modest evidence that the foster parents of children in stable, established placements are at least as reliable as regular parents in reporting their children's mental health difficulties.

Do adolescents in foster care under-report their difficulties more than other adolescents?

I recently came across some studies where the findings suggest the possibility that adolescents in foster care *systematically under-report* their mental health difficulties, in comparison to adolescents at large. I have yet to investigate this formally by way of a systematic review of research evidence, but I think there is sufficient information at hand for me to caution that clinical assessments of adolescents in care should not be based solely on self-reported data.

The first study surveyed the mental health of 326 children and young people aged 6–17 years residing in foster care in a middle-sized Australian city (Sawyer, Carbone, Searle, & Robinson, 2007), using cross-informant Achenbach scales (the parent/caregiver-report CBCL, and for adolescents, the YSR; Achenbach and Rescorla, 2001). While foster-parent-reported CBCL scores were not stratified by age range, 91 adolescents aged 13–17 years completed the YSR, as well as measures of depression and suicidal ideation and behaviour. Sixty-one percent of the all-age sample had CBCL total problems scores in the clinical range, compared to 14% of same-aged Australian children. The former rate is consistent with previous foster-parent-reported CBCL estimates of adolescents in foster care. However, just 35% of adolescent respondents had equivalent self-reported YSR total problem scores in the clinical range, compared to 19% of Australian adolescents. It is unlikely that this discrepancy is accounted for by adolescents in the study having fewer difficulties than younger children, unless there was an adolescent-specific selection bias. It is also notable that the same-aged Australian adolescents reported more difficulties than did their parents. These results suggest the possibility that those adolescents systematically under-reported their difficulties and/or their foster parents systematically over-reported them.

A similar discrepancy was identified in another Australian study, in which a Melbourne clinical service carried out universal assessments of children and young people at entry into care in their region (Milburn, Lynch, & Jackson, 2008). The assessment protocol included SDQs completed by children's foster parents or birth parents, their teachers, and the children themselves if they were adolescents. The rates of SDQ scores that were within the borderline or clinical ranges were 72% as reported by foster parents and birth parents, and 63% as reported by teachers. However, only 33% of adolescent self-reported SDQ scores were in the borderline or clinical ranges.

A third study estimated lifetime and 12-month prevalence rates of DSM-IV mental disorders among a sample of 188 U.S. adolescents aged 14–17 using the Composite International Diagnostic Interview (CIDI; Pecora, White, Jackson, & Wiggins, 2009). These were compared with normative population rates estimated from the same instrument in the U.S. National Comorbidity Study (Adolescent supplement) that were adjusted to match the foster care sample on age, race/ethnicity and gender. The foster care sample had the same 12-month prevalence of any DSM diagnosis as the matched normative sample (35.8% and 36.2%, respectively), while fewer adolescents in foster care had three or more diagnoses than did youths in the matched sample (7.7% vs. 9.1%). In other words, adolescents in foster care were reporting the same rate of clinical-level difficulties as were adolescents at large! This is inconsistent with a very large body of evidence showing that children and young people in care have much higher rates of clinical-level difficulties than do children and young people in the general population. Again, these study findings suggest that adolescents in foster care systematically under-report their difficulties.

A fourth study gathered foster-parent-report and youth self-report SDQ scores for all young people residing in foster care in a single U.S county (N = 138, aged 11–17 years; Jee et al., 2011). Whereas 30% of foster-parent-reported total difficulties scores were in the clinical range, half that rate (16%) of self-reported total difficulties scores were in the clinical range. Interestingly, the highest level of inter-rater agreement was about the presence of clinical-level emotional problems (foster-parent-report = 25%, self-report = 20%), and the lowest agreement was about the presence of conduct problems (foster-parent-report = 38%, self-report = 16%).

Finally, a small longitudinal study of Dutch adolescents in foster care (N = 55) found that while average foster-parent-reported CBCL problem scores *increased* over an 18-month period (the first measure was obtained after 3 months in placement), average self-reported YSR scores *decreased* by around the same magnitude (Strijker, van Oijen, & Knot-Dickscheit, 2011). Without community comparisons we have little way of judging whether this contradiction is accounted for by adolescents under-reporting their difficulties over time, by foster parents over-reporting their child's difficulties over time, or some combination of both. The study found that placement breakdown and mental health severity was associated with greater disagreement between informants (where foster parents tended to score higher, and young people scored lower).

Perhaps in the context of traumatic placement instability, foster parents tend to emphasize the child's difficulties as a way of justifying the placement breakdown, while young people tend to minimize their difficulties (especially conduct problems) for the sake of self-preservation. It also seems logical that some young people are more prepared to disclose their emotional distress to adults than their disruptive or antisocial behaviour. Otherwise, at this stage I am reticent to speculate about why adolescents in care may under-report their difficulties, at least until I have reviewed the research in more detail. However, I think these studies should caution how we interpret a young person's self-reported mental health scores, especially if they report relatively few concerns in the face of contradictory evidence.

In what circumstances, then, should adolescents in alternative care report on their mental health?

If young people residing in alternative care systematically under-report their mental health difficulties, should we still be asking them to report on their mental health, and if so, how can this information be best used and understood? I would argue that there are two strong reasons for not involving young people in routine mental health screening and monitoring by children's agencies, *if it is done without clinical oversight.* The first reason is the one discussed earlier, namely that at a population level, self-reported mental health scores by adolescents in alternative care appear to be unreliable (this of course doesn't mean that every young person's reported scores are unreliable). The second reason is that routine reporting of one's own mental health throughout adolescence, particularly if a young person is not involved with a clinical service, is not a typical adolescent experience. Young people generally have an acute sense of normative adolescent experiences. I firmly believe that we need to do much more to reduce the care system's footprint on these young people's lives – we need to be backing out of their day-to-day lives.

Any young person who is referred for formal assessment is given the opportunity to reveal their mental health difficulties through clinical interviews and self-report questionnaires. But this opportunity only arises if the young person is referred for assessment. The counter-argument to my point of view on this question is that young people's serious mental health problems may *remain undetected* if we don't ask them how they are feeling and thinking – for example, in situations where their caregiver is not aware of the young person's emotional distress. Even though adolescents in care may tend to under-report their difficulties, there will be some instances in which adolescents accurately report clinical-level mental health difficulties that their caregivers are either not aware of or under-report. In other words, in this scenario the young person's mental health difficulties are only detected because they were self-reported. However, Goodman et al.'s (2004) multi-informant screening study of English children in alternative care found that adolescent self-reported SDQ scores identified very few additional clinical cases, beyond those already identified by parents and teachers.

I recommend that children's agencies do not routinely gather self-reported mental health scores from adolescents in care, unless this is done as part of a clinical service, and the adolescents have a good understanding of the purpose and benefits of doing this. Instead, I would recommend that any young person who reports distress or mental health concerns to their caregivers, teachers, social workers, or other young people should be offered the opportunity to describe their concerns in a formal mental health assessment.

Are children's social workers reliable informants?

Our estimations of stability and change in children's mental health not only depend on the intrinsic psychometric properties of the survey measures, but also on who it is that completes those measures at the various time points, and the broader context in which this occurs. Reliability can be reduced due to an informant's lack of knowledge of a child's behaviours, emotions, and thoughts. This translate as non-systematic error (scores are simply less accurate). A number of prospective cohort studies of children in foster care estimated children's mental health from social worker reports (Barber & Delfabbro, 2005; Fanshel & Shinn, 1978; Frank, 1980). However, it is doubtful that social workers have sufficient proximal engagement with children in care to be reliable informants of their mental health, and there is no research supporting the validity of this method.

Q3.   What is doable for children's agencies?

Having spent more than a decade working in a statutory children's agency, I am very aware of the relentless pressure placed on frontline social workers, the difficulty of keeping on top of things, and being forced into reactive rather than proactive ways of working. Clearly, for children's agencies to effectively and consistently screen children's mental health, they need *simple* screening and monitoring protocols that can be implemented without specialized training, and it needs to be *practically doable* – particularly where the agency has no clinically trained professionals on their staff.

Simplicity, and reducing scope for error

Screening and monitoring can be carried out accurately without clinical training if the measures are easy to score and interpret. Ideally, the measures should produce a *single total score* that can be easily and quickly calculated by hand or with an Excel spreadsheet. If calculated by hand, then another person should check the arithmetic before recording the score. The screening decision should be based simply on whether or not the score is at or below the screening cut-point. The measures should require no further interpretation than that.

Don't obtain scores from teachers

When conducting comprehensive assessments of children in care, I have routinely asked teachers to complete checklists and/or provide information about children in an interview. However, this is often problematic, in that teachers are often slow to return checklists or just don't return them at all. Whereas clinicians should include teacher-reported information in their child assessments, I don't believe that teacher-reported data is essential for routine screening and monitoring purposes. More importantly, I think that including teacher-report checklists as part of a routine screening protocol is too impractical for busy children's agencies, because it would require a lot of time and resources to maintain.

Q4.   When and how often should screening and monitoring be done?

Opportunity to provide reliable information about children's mental health

Screening and monitoring measures seek to estimate children's mental health by asking caregivers to report their observations of the presence and frequency of children's symptoms. Whereas some items measure 'externalized' difficulties that can be readily observed by caregivers, others measure difficulties that are less readily observable. These latter symptoms are revealed to caregivers more through children's verbal communication than their non-verbal behaviour. The absence of a clear window to children's inner experiences accounts in large part for poor (typically $r < 0.30$) parent–child inter-rater agreement on cross-informant measures of children's internalizing difficulties (Tarren-Sweeney, Hazell, & Carr, 2004). Given the nature and range of social and emotional difficulties measured by mental health checklists, reliable estimates can only be obtained from caregivers who have had sufficient opportunity to engage and interact closely with the child for a reasonable length of time – so that their reports are not just based on observations of non-verbal behaviour.

Length of time child has resided with their caregiver

In recent years there has been a growing emphasis on assessing children as early as possible after they enter alternate care, with some protocols calling for screening and/or comprehensive assessment in the first weeks of care (Romanelli et al., 2009). While there are good reasons for assessing children's physical and mental health, development, and education status as early as possible, we are less likely to obtain reliable mental health assessment data for children during their first few weeks in a new care placement – whether that be in their initial placement or any subsequent one. We need to be mindful that being removed from one's parents and being placed with caregivers who are strangers is outside the range of normal childhood experience, and that this experience is likely to be bewildering and stressful in the first few weeks – even for children who have moved from an abusive home life to a safe, warm, and caring alternate family. In such a context, many children show a marked reduction in disruptive behaviour in their first few weeks of being cared for by stranger adults (social workers refer to this as a 'honeymoon period'), while others manifest an increased range of symptoms indicative of felt distress, insecurity, anger, and fear.

*Wherever possible, children's mental health should not be screened or monitored until they have resided for **8 weeks** with new foster parents or other caregivers (**and certainly no fewer than 6 weeks**). This advice does not preclude carrying out earlier assessments of children's risk of* causing harm to themselves or others. Where a child's placement has broken down and they are placed with a new foster family without any prior mental health assessment, the agency should ask the child's former (i.e. exiting) foster parents to complete screening measures, rather than new foster parents (i.e. during the first 6 weeks in the new placement).

Frequency of administration

As a general rule, the range of attachment- and trauma-related symptoms typically experienced by children in alternative care are fairly stable over short to medium timeframes, even where children experience radical changes in the developmental conditions that account for those difficulties. For these types of difficulties, the effectiveness of therapeutic caregiving and psychological interventions is likely to be evidenced through gradual symptom reduction over several years rather than dramatic, short-term changes. With this in mind, there is little to be gained from carrying out frequent administrations of screening and monitoring checklists, even during treatment. Frequent administrations are *unlikely* to reveal dramatic changes in scores from one administration to the next, leaving clinicians and agencies with a possibly false impression that an intervention or placement is not therapeutic.

In instances where children are in stable, long-term adoptive, foster or kinship placements, there is little to be gained from screening or monitoring children's mental health more than once per year. Yearly re-administration provides greater scope for reliably detecting meaningful changes in children's mental health than more frequent administrations, especially when checklists are completed by the same caregiver.

Aside from routine screening and monitoring carried out by children's agencies, clinicians may see benefit in more frequent re-assessment and monitoring – for example, when children and/or their caregivers are receiving intensive psychological interventions (such as Treatment Foster Care), or when children experience a change of placement. However, clinicians should be mindful that the absence of meaningful change in symptom scores over 6-month or shorter timeframes provides a less reliable indication of the course of children's mental health difficulties, than a similar result measured over a 12-month timeframe.

Q5. What situations can bias caregivers' reports of children's mental health?

Estimations of the accuracy of screening measures (such as the AUC) and of the reliability of other types of monitoring and assessment measures are typically obtained for a single, homogenous class of informants (e.g. parents), as well as a homogenous context. Typically these data are gathered solely for research, a context that is unlikely to generate systematic respondent bias. Occasionally however, these data may be gathered in a real-world clinical context, where research is a secondary purpose for gathering the data. In this situation, the context may well account for systematic respondent bias. For example, if scores are collected as part of an initial intake assessment to CAMHS, foster parents may over-report children's difficulties so as to increase the chance that their child will receive a service. Therefore, we need to be mindful that published research estimates of screening accuracy and reliability may not apply to some real-world contexts.

What situations can lead to systematic over-reporting of children's mental health difficulties?

There are a number of situations in which foster parents, kinship carers, and adoptive parents may over-report children's difficulties. The respondents can overstate or exaggerate children's problems, consciously or unconsciously. The effects can be somewhat subtle – for example tending to rate symptoms as occurring 'often' more than 'sometimes'.

The most common circumstance in which children's difficulties are overstated is when caregivers are desperate to receive clinical support, and they worry about whether or not their child's scores will be high enough for them to be accepted by the service. From my perspective, I don't see this situation as causing a problem. We know how central placement stability is to these children's longer-term development and well-being, including their mental health. My feeling is that in a circumstance where a foster parent is convinced that their foster child has a mental health problem requiring therapeutic support, and they are desperate to obtain that support for their child, then this is a placement that is under stress – it warrants comprehensive assessment on the strength of that information alone.

A more troubling situation arises where the level and severity of children's mental health difficulties are linked within the children's agency to *factors other than* gaining access to a clinical service. These include linking higher developmental problems to higher rates of fostering payments and gaining access to additional disability payments. Similarly, where the level and severity of children's mental health difficulties are tied to the provision of respite care and other tangible support services, caregivers may feel compelled to overstate children's difficulties, particularly if reporting lower scores may result in a loss of payments or supports. I can't suggest a good remedy for this situation, other than that agencies should avoid linking payment and support decisions to scores on checklists.

What situations can lead to systematic **under-reporting** of children's mental health difficulties?

In some circumstances, caregivers may feel impelled to under-report their children's difficulties because they wish to maintain the impression that 'all is well' with the child's development and placement. This may occur, for example, when foster parents are awaiting approval of an adoption order, or when foster parents tire of social workers intruding into their family lives.

I have personally been involved in several cases where caregivers have grossly under-reported their children's mental health difficulties, and have generally tried to hide from agencies and clinicians the extent of the child's difficulties. This typically occurs because the caregiver fears having the child(ren) removed from their care, and they fear that their child's mental health difficulties may be cited as evidence of incompetent caregiving. In most of these cases the caregivers were the children's biological grandparents, many of whom had earlier involvement with child welfare services in relation to their own children. In other words, while these kinship caregivers had placements that were approved by the statutory agency, they nevertheless perceived that their caregiving was being scrutinized (which sometimes was the case).

What situations can result in **generally inaccurate** *reporting of children's mental health difficulties?*

There are some situations that can introduce what psychometricians refer to as *random error*. This is error that isn't biased in a particular direction; it's just general inaccuracy. One common reason for scores being generally inaccurate is that the respondents don't take sufficient time or care to faithfully answer the questions. This typically occurs when respondents don't really want to complete the checklist but feel compelled to do so. Their disinclination can be tied to a belief that the scores are not used for good purpose ("it's a waste of time"). We sometimes see this when an adolescent feels compelled to participate in an assessment, and they complete a checklist without actually reading the questions; they just randomly tick boxes. Foster parents can also take less care in completing a measure if they don't see it as important. While we rarely experience this in clinical assessments, I suspect that routine mandatory administration of mental health checklists (such as annual SDQ reporting required by law in the United Kingdom) prompts a small proportion of respondents to complete checklists hastily (as they don't see this as being a useful exercise).

A second situation that reduces the general accuracy of checklist scores is caregiver reading ability. Items and instructions on child mental health checklists are generally written for a reading age of around 10 or 12 years. Increasingly, children in statutory care are placed with grandparents and other kin, and this group of caregivers are more likely to have had a disrupted education. I have also met quite a number of older foster parents who left school at a young age and don't have a functional reading age.

Q6.   Which measures should agencies use?

Ages 12 months to 35 months

My reviews of the BITSEA and ASQ:SE suggest that the BITSEA is the best option for screening for this age group. The BITSEA is the more accurate screener for use with infants and toddlers in the general community. Furthermore, one study found that the ASQ:SE was insufficiently accurate in screening for mental health problems of infants in foster care (Hillen & Gafson, 2014). However, the one caveat is that as yet there has been no research on the BITSEA's screening accuracy with an in-care population. While the BITSEA was derived from the ITSEA for the purpose of screening, its psychometric properties are sufficient for it to be used as a monitoring measure as well. Agencies can also use the BITSEA without clinical oversight.

If agencies don't see the need to screen children from such a young age, then the SDQ can be used with children as young as 30 months (although it has only been researched with children in care from 36 months).

Ages 36 months to 47 months

I recommend that agencies use the SDQ for both mental health screening and monitoring purposes in this age range. In the future I am hoping that preschool versions of the Assessment Checklist measures (Assessment Checklist for Preschoolers [ACP; ACP-SF] and Brief Assessment Checklist for Preschoolers [BAC-P]) will be available to use alongside the SDQ. These are presently under development, but are some way off being ready to distribute.

Ages 4–17 years

Monitoring

With regards to mental health *monitoring* for school-aged children and adolescents, the SDQ provides valid and reliable monitoring of general mental health problems, while the BAC monitors children's attachment- and trauma-related difficulties. Agencies can employ both of these measures without clinical oversight.

However, clinicians wishing to carry out treatment monitoring will obtain better information from using the ACC-SF and ACA-SF in place of the BAC-C and BAC-A, respectively. Furthermore, where clinicians included the CBCL in a child's psychological assessment, there are advantages to using the BPM (derived from the CBCL) in their treatment monitoring rather than the SDQ.

Screening

With regards to mental health *screening* for school-aged children and adolescents, the SDQ and BAC demonstrate comparable screening accuracy in foster care research samples. While the SDQ and BAC are both accurate screeners for this population, the SDQ is a little more accurate in detecting general mental health problems (internalizing, externalizing, and attentional problems), while the BAC is more accurate in detecting attachment- and trauma-related psychopathology that is characteristic of children with a history of maltreatment (Tarren-Sweeney et al., in press).

Q7.   What are the optimal screening cut-points for the SDQ and BAC?

The *classic approach to screening* is to employ it as the first stage of a two-stage or multi-stage assessment strategy. The aim of the first (i.e. screening) stage is to locate as many cases as possible. The aim of the second and subsequent assessment stages is to rule out as many non-cases as possible. Therefore, when screening is the first stage of a two- or multi-stage assessment process, sensitivity is more important than specificity (except where there are seriously adverse social or emotional consequences for false positive screening, e.g. for a life-threatening illness). There are several reasons why this is particularly true for children in alternative care. First, the implications for children growing in care with undetected mental health problems are more serious than they are for children who don't have clinical-level problems being subjected to a second-stage assessment. Second, while false positive screens are likely to be correctly identified as non-cases during their second-stage assessment, there is no such remedy for false negative screens; they stay undetected. Finally, because children in care have such high prevalence of clinical level mental health difficulties (above 50%), loss of specificity within this population translates as fewer false positive screens and higher positive predictive value (the proportion of positive screens who are true cases) than occurs with mental health screening of children and young people in the general community.

The published SDQ clinical range cut-points favour specificity over sensitivity. The results of the recent survey of the mental health of Dutch foster children (Goemans, Tarren-Sweeney, van Geel, & Vedder, 2017), which included both SDQ and BAC measures, suggested that the SDQ screening cut-points have insufficient sensitivity with this population, that is they are set too high – *but also*, that the BAC screening cut-point that I previously recommended has insufficient specificity, that is it is set too low. This prompted myself and several other researchers to re-evaluate the cut-points on both measures, with a view to proposing improved cut-points for children in alternative care, that preference sensitivity over specificity. We did this by comparing BAC with SDQ screening statistics across three national studies: the Australian CICS surveys, the Dutch survey, and a recent survey of clinic-referred English children adopted from care (an evaluation of the new Adoption Support Fund; Tarren-Sweeney et al., in press). While the Dutch and English surveys collected BAC and SDQ scores, the CICS surveys collected ACC/ACA and CBCL scores. Given the BAC items were all derived from the longer-form ACC and ACA, BAC scores were readily calculated for the CICS samples. We located a set of CBCL items that provided a reasonable approximation of the SDQ items that constitute the SDQ total difficulties scale, and generated a 'SDQ proxy' score for the CICS samples.

Extracting further accuracy through using the BAC and SDQ in combination

In addition to identifying optimal cut-points for the SDQ and BAC, these analyses compared the screening accuracy of the following three methods:

1 SDQ alone
2 BAC alone
3 Using the SDQ and BAC *in parallel* (i.e. scoring above the cut-point on either measure results in a positive screen).

A summary of the various ROC analyses is provided in Table 5.1, along with the sensitivity and specificity rates for the new optimal

Table 5.1 Sensitivity and specificity of four BAC/SDQ screening strategies: BAC, SDQ, combined BAC-SDQ score, and BAC-SDQ used in parallel[a]

	Cut-point	Dutch sample			Australian sample													English sample[c]
		Intervention			High carer stress			Intervention			ACC/ACA clinical range			CBCL clinical range			ACC/ACA or CBCL clinical range			
		AUC	Sens.	Spec.	AUC	Sens.	Spec.	AUC	Sens.	Spec.	AUC	Sens.	Spec.	AUC	Sens.	Spec.	AUC	Sens.	Spec.	Sens.
Children																				
BAC-C	7+	.72	85%	45%	.79	92%	46%	.75	72%	72%	.99	100%	75%	.92	93%	72%	.96	94%	80%	97%
SDQ/SDQ-proxy[b]	10+	.77	80%	55%	.79	85%	52%	.80	78%	71%	.90	94%	63%	.96	99%	69%	.94	94%	72%	97%
BAC-C *or* SDQ parallel screening	BAC 8+/ SDQ 11+		85%	52%		92%	52%		79%	66%		100%	63%		99%	65%		99%	72%	98%
Adolescents																				
BAC-A	7+	.76	86%	45%	.87	95%	48%	.78	63%	70%	.99	99%	75%	.94	94%	74%	.97	94%	81%	99%
SDQ/SDQ proxy[b]	10+	.77	84%	62%	.83	90%	63%	.79	65%	81%	.93	97%	78%	.97	89%	87%	.97	95%	85%	99%
BAC-C *or* SDQ parallel screening	BAC 8+/ SDQ 11+		88%	48%		98%	52%		69%	75%		99%	71%		100%	73%		99%	80%	100%

[a] Data originally published in Tarren-Sweeney et al. (in press).

[b] Refers to SDQ scores obtained in the Dutch and English surveys, and 'SDQ-proxy' scores derived from CBCL scores obtained in the Australian surveys.

[c] The English sample was clinic-referred child adoptees from statutory care. As they were all designated to be clinical cases, sensitivity can be calculated, but specificity is not applicable.

cut-points. These analyses showed that while the BAC and SDQ had comparable accuracy when used alone, the highest accuracy was gained from employing the two measures in parallel and raising the cut-points for both measures by one point.

Recommended procedure – SDQ and BAC administered together

The recommended procedure is to have caregivers complete the SDQ and BAC measures simultaneously, and to refer children for a comprehensive mental health assessment if *either* their SDQ total difficulties score is *11 or higher or* their BAC score is *8 or higher*. The present analyses indicate that this procedure is highly accurate at identifying children in alternative care with clinical-level mental health difficulties (including attachment- and trauma-related difficulties), with very few such children remaining undetected. This procedure also achieves very high sensitivity (true positive detection rate) while retaining acceptable specificity.

Alternative procedure – SDQ or BAC used as sole screening measures

Alternatively, where children's agencies are unable or unwilling to employ our recommended parallel screening procedure, and only wish to use a single measure, *acceptable* screening accuracy is achieved when caregivers complete either the SDQ or BAC measures. If the SDQ is used, refer children for a comprehensive mental health assessment if their SDQ total difficulties score is *10 or higher*. If the BAC is used, refer children for a comprehensive mental health assessment if their BAC-C or BAC-A score is *7 or higher*.

Note

These cut-points were selected to *preference sensitivity over specificity*, on the understanding that with this population, the benefits of detecting children who need therapeutic services outweighs the costs of assessing additional children who are later found to not require therapeutic services. Nevertheless, agencies should be aware that a fair number of children who score above these cut-points will be 'false positives'.

Summary

This chapter sets out a simple protocol for mental screening and monitoring that children's agencies can implement with or without clinical oversight. The key details are summarized in Table 5.2.

Table 5.2 A protocol for mental health screening and monitoring with children in alternative care: summary points

---

1. Automatically refer for specialist assessment (bypass screening)
All of the following children should bypass screening and be assessed by specialist clinical and/or developmental services:

- Children with moderate or severe intellectual disability
- Children entering residential care
- Children experiencing a placement disruption.

2. Timeframes for routine screening and monitoring

- Universal screening *8 weeks* (certainly *no earlier than 6 weeks*) following entry into alternative care or a new placement
- If mental health assessment needs to occur before 6 weeks, have former caregiver complete measures
- Monitor every 12 months thereafter, unless a change of placement prompts earlier re-assessment.

3. Recommended measures for routine mental health screening and monitoring without clinical oversight

- For 1- and 2-year-olds (12 months to 35 months), *use the parent form of the* BITSEA[a]
- For 3-year-olds (36 months to 47 months), *use the 2- to 4-year-old parent form of the* SDQ[b]
- For 4- to 11-year-olds, *use the 4- to 17-year-old parent form of the* SDQ[c] *and the* BAC-C[d]
- For 12- to 17-year-olds, *use the 4- to 17-year-old parent form of the* SDQ[c] *and the* BAC-A.[d]

4. Recommended SDQ **and** BAC-C/BAC-A **screening cut-points for ages 4–17**

- If child's caregiver fills out **both** the BAC and the SDQ (the preferred method), refer the child for a comprehensive clinical assessment if their BAC score is *8* or higher *OR* their SDQ score is *11* or higher
- If child's caregiver only fills out the BAC (an acceptable method), refer the child for a comprehensive clinical assessment if their BAC score is *7* or higher
- If child's caregiver only fills out the SDQ (an acceptable method), refer the child for a comprehensive clinical assessment if their SDQ score is *10* or higher.

(*Continued*)

Table 5.2 (Continued)

---

5. Recommended measures for monitoring 4- to 17-year-olds' mental health by *clinicians* following a comprehensive assessment

- If the comprehensive assessment included the ACC or ACA, use the ACC-SF and ACC+ (4- to 11-year-olds) or ACA-SF and ACA+ (for 12- to 17-year-olds)[e] for post-assessment or treatment monitoring (in place of the BAC-C and BAC-A)
- If the comprehensive assessment included the CBCL, use the BPM for post-assessment and/or treatment monitoring (in place of the SDQ).

---

a Purchase the BITSEA Pearson Clinical at www.pearsonclinical.com.au/products/view/56.
b Download the 'One-sided *SDQ* for parents or educators of 2–4 year olds' at www.sdqinfo.com/py/sdqinfo/b0.py.
c Download the 'One-sided *SDQ* for parents or teachers of 4–17 year olds' at www.sdqinfo.com/py/sdqinfo/b0.py.
d Download the *BAC-C* and *BAC-A* at http://childpsych.org.uk/downloadBAC.html.
e Clinicians can view information on how to register and receive these measures at http://childpsych.org.uk/.

References

Achenbach, T., & Edelbrock, C. (1986). *Manual for the Teacher's Report Form and teacher version of the Child Behavior Profile*. Burlington: University of Vermont.

Achenbach, T., & Rescorla, L. (2001). *Manual for ASEBA school-age forms and profiles*. Burlington: University of Vermont, Research Center for Children, Youth, & Families.

Barber, J., & Delfabbro, P. (2005). Children's adjustment to long-term foster care. *Children and Youth Services Review, 27*, 329–340.

Conners, C. K. (2008). *Conners comprehensive behavior rating scales manual*. Toronto, ON: Multi-Health Systems.

Einfeld, S., & Tonge. (1995). The developmental behavior checklist: The development and validation of an instrument to assess behavioral and emotional disturbance in children and adolescents with mental retardation. *Journal of Autism & Developmental Disorders, 25*(2), 81–104.

Fanshel, D., & Shinn, E. (1978). *Children in foster care: A longitudinal investigation*. New York, NY: Columbia University Press.

Frank, G. (1980). Treatment needs of children in foster care. *American Journal of Orthopsychiatry, 50*(2), 256–263.

Garland, A., Landsverk, J., Hough, R., & Ellis-Macleod, E. (1996). Type of maltreatment as a predictor of mental health service use for children in foster care. *Child Abuse & Neglect, 20*(8), 675–688.

Goemans, A., Tarren-Sweeney, M., van Geel, M., & Vedder, P. (2017). Psychosocial screening and monitoring for children in foster care: Psychometric properties of the Brief Assessment Checklists in a Dutch population study. *Clinical Child Psychology & Psychiatry*, 1–16. https://doi.org/10.1177/1359104517706527

Goodman, R. (2001). Psychometric properties of the Strengths and Difficulties Questionnaire. *Journal of the American Academy of Child & Adolescent Psychiatry*, *40*, 1337–1345.

Goodman, R., Ford, T., Corbin, T., & Meltzer, H. (2004). Using the Strengths and Difficulties Questionnaire (SDQ) multi-informant algorithm to screen looked-after children for psychiatric disorders. *European Child and Adolescent Psychiatry, 13*(Suppl 2), 25–31.

Halfon, N., Mendonca, A., & Berkowitz, G. (1995). Health status of children in foster care: The experience of the Center for the Vulnerable Child. *Archives of Pediatrics & Adolescent Medicine, 149*(4), 386–392.

Hillen, T., & Gafson, L. (2014). Statutory health assessments for pre-school foster children fail to screen accurately for mental health disorders. *Clinical Child Psychology & Psychiatry, 19*(2), 313–327.

Jee, S., Szilagyi, M., Conn, A., Nilsen, W., Toth, S., Baldwin, C., & Szilagyi, G. (2011). Validating office-based screening for psychosocial strengths and difficulties among youths in foster care. *Pediatrics, 127*(5), 904–910.

McConaughy, S., Stanger, C., & Achenbach, T. (1992). Three-year course of behavioral/emotional problems in a national sample of 4- to 16-year-olds: I. Agreement among informants. *Journal of the American Academy of Child & Adolescent Psychiatry, 31*(5), 932–940.

Milburn, N., Lynch, M., & Jackson, J. (2008). Early identification of mental health needs for children in care: A therapeutic assessment programme for statutory clients of child protection. *Clinical Child Psychology and Psychiatry, 13*(1), 31–47.

Pecora, P., White, C., Jackson, L., & Wiggins, T. (2009). Mental health of current and former recipients of foster care: A review of recent studies in the USA. *Child & Family Social Work, 14*, 132–146.

Romanelli, L., Landsverk, J., Levitt, J., Leslie, L. K., Hurley, M., Bellonci, C., . . . Pecora, P. J. (2009). Best practices for mental health in child welfare: Screening, assessment, and treatment guidelines. *Child Welfare, 88*(1), 163–188.

Sawyer, M., Baghurst, P., & Clark, J. (1992). Differences between reports from children, parents and teachers: Implications for epidemiological studies. *Australian & New Zealand Journal of Psychiatry, 26*(4), 652–660.

Sawyer, M., Carbone, J., Searle, A., & Robinson, P. (2007). The mental health and well-being of children and adolescents in home-based foster care. *Medical Journal of Australia, 186*, 181–184.

Smith, S. (2007). Making sense of multiple informants in child and adolescent psychopathology. *Journal of Psychoeducational Assessment, 25*(2), 139–149.

Strijker, J., van Oijen, S., & Knot-Dickscheit, J. (2011). Assessment of problem behaviour by foster parents and their foster children. *Child & Family Social Work, 16*, 93–100.

Tarren-Sweeney, M. (2014). *Clinician's guide to the Assessment Checklist series: Specialized mental health measures for children in care.* London: Routledge.

Tarren-Sweeney, M., Goemans, A., van Geel, M., Vedder, P., Hahne, A. S., & Gieve, M. (in press). Mental health screening for children in care using the Strengths and Difficulties Questionnaire and the Brief Assessment Checklists: Guidance from three national studies. *Developmental Child Welfare.*

Tarren-Sweeney, M., Hazell, P., & Carr, V. (2004). Are foster parents reliable informants of children's behaviour problems? *Child: Care, Health and Development, 30*(2), 167–175.

Verhulst, F. C., & Akkerhuis, G. W. (1989). Agreement between parents' and teachers' ratings of behavioral/emotional problems of children aged 4–12. *Journal of Child Psychology & Psychiatry & Allied Disciplines, 30*(1), 123–136.

Verhulst, F. C., & Van der Ende, J. (1991). Assessment of child psychopathology: Relationships between different methods, different informants and clinical judgment of severity. *Acta Psychiatrica Scandinavica, 84*(2), 155–159.

6 Is screening and brief monitoring enough?

The case for universal, comprehensive assessment of children in statutory care (including those transitioning to legally permanent alternative care)

This book's main purpose is to promote universal, periodic screening and monitoring of children's mental health by the agencies that hold statutory parental responsibility for them. The reason for doing so is to improve the detection of clinical-level difficulties among these children, as detection is presently haphazard and unsatisfactory, and a considerable proportion of affected children thus miss out on much-needed therapeutic services. However, while this would represent a big improvement on the status quo, I don't see it as the optimal solution. We should be mindful that for this population of children, universal mental health screening *is not best practice*. Rather, it is best practice *within the present constraints of limited mental health resources*.

What then would constitute best practice? In this chapter I propose that, given the availability of an adequately trained and specialized clinical workforce, children in alternative care would be best served by *universal, comprehensive assessment* by clinicians with specialized knowledge and skills, in what I term clinical/psychosocial-developmental scope of practice.

What is wrong with regular child and adolescent mental health services?

Chapter 2 provides some of the context and detail for why regular child and mental health services, operating within an acute care model, are not well matched to the developmental and clinical needs of children in alternative care. The most visible shortcoming in the provision of mental health services for children in care, as well as those adopted from care (Sturgess & Selwyn, 2007), is insufficient capacity. This is despite these populations having high rates of service use relative to other disadvantaged children (Bellamy, Traube, & Gopalan, 2010; Sturgess & Selwyn, 2007). The prevalence of clinically significant mental health difficulties among these children is sufficiently high to warrant systematic assessment of their mental health service needs. Yet it is unlikely that any state or country could sustain a 'whole of population' approach to detection and management of mental health difficulties among children in care without a large expansion of service capacity – regardless of whether the work is done by specialist alternate care teams or generic child mental health services. It is known, for example, that U.S. children in care receive a disproportionate share of Medicaid public mental health services relative to other disadvantaged child populations with high prevalence of mental health difficulties (Leslie et al., 2005), including maltreated children who remain in parental care.

Beyond questions of scale and capacity, it is apparent that publicly funded, 'acute care' child and adolescent mental health services are poorly matched to the service needs of a disadvantaged child population presenting with complex attachment- and trauma-related psychopathology, and unstable living arrangements. Such children require greater continuity and certainty of care than acute care services are designed to provide. This requirement seems particularly ill-matched to acute care services that function within a 'managed care' environment (Leslie, Kelleher, Burns, Landsverk, & Rolls, 2003) or which are required to achieve high client turnover.

Standard child clinical conceptualization, assessment methods, and formulations miss the mark for these vulnerable populations in a number of critical ways. This is partly indicative of knowledge gaps in our research. However, a lot has also been learned that is yet to be translated into standard clinical practice, including knowledge and skills that can increase clinicians' understanding of these children, and yield more accurate clinical formulations. In the main these have quite a specialized focus, requiring fairly detailed or intensive training. For this reason, it is more realistic to set our sights on developing specialized clinical workforces for child welfare work than expanding the scope of standard clinical training.

The remedy: build specialized services with sufficient capacity to assess all children in statutory care

What then should be the main characteristics of specialized clinical practice with these populations? First, it should be guided by appropriate conceptual frameworks for formulating complex attachment- and trauma-related disorders, and the biopsychosocial mechanisms and developmental pathways that determine the mental health of children with a history of care and/or maltreatment. The significance of early social adversity and attachment conditions on these populations' neurological and psychological development points to complex, time-sensitive etiological mechanisms. For these children more than others, it is essential that we incorporate new knowledge from developmental psychopathology research, and an ecological-transactional framework (e.g. Cicchetti, Toth, & Maughan 2000), into clinical reasoning and case hypothesis generation.

Second, in addition to ecological enquiry, specialized clinical practice requires an improved conceptualization of complex attachment- and trauma-related symptomatology manifested by these children (DeJong, 2010). While some work has been devoted to re-conceptualizing such difficulties (Crittenden, 1997; O'Connor & Zeanah, 2003; van der Kolk, 2005), it may be several decades before we attain an empirically validated classification of attachment- and trauma-related mental health difficulties that accommodates a high degree of symptom complexity. Until that eventuates, I believe that specialized clinical practice requires both an understanding of the particular limitations of present diagnostic classifications in relation to these forms of psychopathology, and some modification of clinical reasoning and formulation to work around these limitations.

A third characteristic pertains to the *comprehensiveness* of clinical assessments. Specialized practice with these populations requires more detailed assessment of attachment- and trauma-related problems, and a wider developmental and contextual focus than that typically employed in mental health clinical assessments. In essence, specialized assessments of these children requires a shift from a relatively narrow, 'mechanical' focus on identifying children's symptoms and disorders – to seeking a comprehensive understanding of children's felt experience, their relationships, family/placement processes, and systemic and care-related influences on children's lives. We need to extend clinical assessments beyond the individual child, to include assessment of the adoptive/foster/kinship family systems, and how these systems are influenced by child welfare systemic factors. Clinicians need to enquire about motivations for caregiving and systemic influences on carer roles (Dozier, Grasso, Lindheim, & Lewis, 2007), caregiver attachment styles (Schofield & Beek, 2005), and caregiver 'felt security' regarding the permanence of their relationships with the subject child. This is because the primary therapeutic agent for children in alternative care is their substitute family (Schofield & Beek, 2005).

Clinical/psychosocial-developmental scope of practice

The characteristics of specialized clinical practice set out earlier translate first as increased expertise in the assessment and formulation of attachment- and trauma-related psychopathology among child welfare populations. It also involves a shift beyond the traditional boundaries of clinical practice to include much greater focus on the nature of family life that sustains and promotes the development of children who have experienced chronic social adversity; children's felt experiences and worldview; child welfare systemic influences; and more detailed consideration of children's developmental histories, with particular reference to attachment and trauma theories.

Together this represents a *clinical/psychosocial-developmental* scope of practice that is specific to the development and well-being of child welfare clients, and most particularly to children who are in (or have exited from) alternate care. Clinical/psychosocial-developmental practice is thus as much focussed on the minutiae of context as it is with identifying and treating mental health difficulties. It requires the clinician to have a good understanding of age-sensitive psychosocial effects of such things as loss, entry into impermanent care, placement changes, restoration to parental care, length and types of court orders, sibling co-placement, birth family contact, and adoption from care by existing foster parents versus strangers. It also directs clinicians to enquire about the nature and quality of care that children receive in their present placements, and to learn (where possible) about children's care experiences in previous placements. I believe these factors collectively have greater proximal influence on children's development than do individual clinical interventions. Clinical/psychosocial-developmental practice thus seeks to facilitate therapeutic change and prevent the onset of additional psychopathology by influencing decisions made by social care agencies, courts, and caregivers. This consultation role is as central to clinical work with this population, as is the formulation of their treatment plans. Clinical/psychosocial-developmental practice also sets out to provide a better platform for conducting psychosocial interventions within the adoptive/foster/kinship family than standard child clinical practice.

How might *all* children in statutory care benefit from a comprehensive clinical/psychosocial-developmental assessment?

Almost all children in care are exposed to systemic, adverse pressures on their development and well-being, and they have vulnerabilities that are not necessarily revealed by their mental health presentations. Many of these pressures can be profoundly distressing and undermine children's felt security. Much of this risk can be identified and intercepted, and their effects prevented and remediated, through specialized assessment. Such assessment includes a wider developmental and contextual focus than that typically employed in mental health clinical assessments. In essence, specialized assessment of these children requires a shift from a relatively narrow, 'mechanical' focus on identifying children's symptoms and disorders to seeking a comprehensive understanding of their felt experience, their relationships, family/placement processes, and systemic and care-related pressures on their development. In other words, these assessments don't just compartmentalize children's mental health difficulties as health problems requiring conventional treatment. Instead, they locate children's mental health within their broader social contexts – information that is fundamental to *developmental child welfare* practice.

References

Bellamy, J., Traube, D., & Gopalan, G. (2010). A national study of the impact of outpatient mental health services for children in long-term foster care. *Clinical Child Psychology and Psychiatry, 15*(4), 467–480.

Cicchetti, D., Toth, S. L., & Maughan, A. (2000). An ecological-transactional model of child maltreatment. In A. Sameroff & M. Lewis (Eds.), *Handbook of developmental psychopathology* (2nd ed., pp. 689–722). Dordrecht, Netherlands: Kluwer Academic.

Crittenden, P. (1997). Toward an integrative theory of trauma: A dynamic-maturation approach. In D. Cicchetti & S. L. Toth (Eds.), *Developmental perspectives on trauma: Theory, research, and intervention: Rochester symposium on developmental psychology* (Vol. 8, pp. 33–84). Rochester, NY: University of Rochester Press.

DeJong, M. (2010). Some reflections on the use of psychiatric diagnosis in the looked after or 'in care' child population. *Clinical Child Psychology and Psychiatry, 15*(4), 589–599.

Dozier, M., Grasso, D., Lindheim, O., & Lewis, E. (2007). The role of caregiver commitment in foster care: Insights from the This Is My Baby Interview. In D. Oppenheim & D. Goldsmith (Eds.), *Attachment theory in clinical work with children: Bridging the gap between research and practice* (pp. 90–108). New York, NY: Guilford Press.

Leslie, L., Hurlburt, M., James, S., Landsverk, J., Slymen, D., & Zhang, J. (2005). Relationship between entry into child welfare and mental health service use. *Psychiatric Services, 56*(8), 981–987.

Leslie, L., Kelleher, K., Burns, B., Landsverk, J., & Rolls, J. (2003). Foster care and Medicaid managed care. *Child Welfare, 82*(3), 367–392.

O'Connor, T., & Zeanah, C. (2003). Current perspectives on attachment disorders: Rejoinder and synthesis. *Attachment and Human Development, 5*(3), 321–326.

Schofield, G., & Beek, M. (2005). Providing a secure base: Parenting children in long-term foster family care. *Attachment and Human Development, 7*(1), 3–25.

Sturgess, W., & Selwyn, J. (2007). Supporting the placements of children adopted out of care. *Clinical Child Psychology and Psychiatry, 12*(1), 13–28.

van der Kolk, B. (2005). Developmental trauma disorder. *Psychiatric Annals, 35*(5), 401–408.

Appendix 1

Assessment Checklist for Children Short Form (ACC-SF) girls' profile sheet

ACC-SF Assessment Checklist for Children – Short Form

Girls Profile Sheet (2012 version) Reference group: 5-10 year-old girls in long-term alternate care

© 2004 Michael Tarren-Sweeney, PhD www.childpsych.org.uk

Add scale scores

I ___
II ___
III ___
IV ___
V ___
VI ___
VII ___
VIII ___
IX ___

Total Clinical Score ___
(Transfer total score to next page)

T score ranges shown: ≥72, 70, 65, 60, 55, 50, ≤43

* Boxes show the percentile range for zero scores.

SHORT-FORM CLINICAL SCALES

I SEXUAL BEHAVIOUR	II PSEUDOMATURE	III NON-RECIPROCAL	IV INDISCRIMINATE	V INSECURE	VI ANXIOUS – DISTRUSTFUL	VII ABNORMAL PAIN RESPONSE	VIII FOOD MAINTENANCE	IX SELF – INJURY
35. Describes / imitates	21. Precocious	2. Avoid eye contact	1. Attention-seeking	4. Clingy	5. Distrusts adults	6. Does not cry	9. Eats too much	33. Bites self
37. Forces / Pressures	22. Prefers adults	7. Doesn't share	3. Changes friends	12. Career rejection	10. Fears men	19. Laughs if hurt	13. Gorges food	34. Self-injury
40. Age-inappropriate	23. Prefer older kids	8. Affectionless	15. Hugs men	16. Peer rejection	11. Fears bed-time	36. Pain not shown	14. Hides food	39. Head-banging
42. Touches others	28. Independent	18. Non-empathic	24. Strangers as family	25. Insecure	17. Fears harm	44. Won't say if hurt	26. Steals food	41. Threatens self-injury
43. Tries to initiate sex	29. Role reversal	20. Manipulative	27. Friendly strangers	32. Worries for career	31. Wary or vigilant			
		30. Uncaring			38. Panic attacks			

Total I	Total II	Total III	Total IV	Total V	Total VI	Total VII	Total VIII	Total IX
___	___	___	___	___	___	___	___	___

The ACC-SF checklist and profile sheet © 2004 are copyright of the author. Restrictions on the use of the ACC are listed in the accompanying limited licence. Unauthorised copying or distribution of paper or electronic forms is illegal.

ACC-SF Assessment Checklist for Children – Short Form   Girls Profile Sheet (2012 version)

© 2004 Michael Tarren-Sweeney, PhD   www.childpsych.org.uk

Reference group: 5-10 year-old girls in long-term alternate care

---

ID:

Child's Name:

	Year	Month	Day
Date of Birth:			
Date of Assessment:			
Age:			

Carer's name:
(the person who completed the ACC)

Carer's gender: Female ☐ Male ☐

Length of time carer has known child: _____

Carer's relationship to child
☐ Birth parent
☐ Step-parent
☐ Grandparent
☐ Other relative
☐ Adoptive parent
☐ Foster parent
☐ Group home staff
☐ Large residential staff
☐ Youth worker
☐ Other (describe): _____

Care Status
☐ Not in care (resides with parents)
☐ Adoption
☐ Kinship care (resides with relatives)
☐ Permanent or long-term foster care
☐ Temporary or short-term foster care
☐ Group or residential care
☐ Other (describe): _____

Referral Details:

Total Clinical Score =

Raw	T	%ile
	Clinical range	
52-88	≥72	≥99
50-51	71	98
48-49	70	98
46-47	69	97
44-46	68	96
42-43	67	96
40-41	66	95
38-39	65	93
37	64	92
36	63	90
35	62	88
33-34	61	86
31-32	60	84
29-30	59	82
26-28	58	79
22-25	57	76
20-21	56	73
18-19	55	69
16-17	54	66
14-15	53	62
	52	58
	Borderline clinical range	
13	52	58
11-12	51	54
10	50	50
	Normal range	
9	49	46
8	48	42
7	47	38
6	46	34
	45	31
5	44	27
	43	24
4	42	21
	41	18
3	40	16
	39	14
	38	12
2	37	10
	36	8
	35	7
1	34	5
	33	4
	32	4
0	31	3
	30	2
	29	2
	≤28	1

The ACC-SF checklist and profile sheet © 2004 are copyright of the author. Restrictions on the use of the ACC are listed in the accompanying limited licence. Unauthorised copying or distribution of paper or electronic forms is illegal.

Appendix 2

Assessment Checklist for Adolescents
Short Form (ACA-SF) profile sheet

ACA-SF Assessment Checklist for Adolescents – Short Form   Profile Sheet (boys & girls)

© 2012 Michael Tarren-Sweeney, PhD   www.childpsych.org.uk

	I	II	III	IV	V	VI	TOTAL	
	6-12	8-16	5-14	6-12	8-10	5-10	18-74	*Marked*
CLINICAL ↑	3-5	5-7	3-4	4-5	6-7	3-4	12-17	*Indicated*
	2	3-4	2	2-3	4-5	1-2	9-11	*Elevated*
SUB-CLINICAL ↓	0-1	0-2	0-1	0-1	0-3	0	0-8	*Normative*

CLINICAL SCALES

I NON-RECIPROCAL	II SOCIAL INSTABILITY	III EMOTIONAL DYSREGULATION / DISTORTED SOCIAL COGNITION	IV DISSOCIATION / TRAUMA SYMPTOMS	V FOOD MAINTENANCE BEHAVIOUR	VI SEXUAL BEHAVIOUR
2 Affectionless	1 Craves affection	15 Friends against	22 Dazed	3 Eats secretly	27 Forces / Pressures
6 Hides feelings	8 Impulsive	17 Startles easily	24 Real or dream?	4 Eats too much	31 Shows genitals
12 Refuses to talk	9 Precocious	23 Scary thoughts	26 Things aren't real	5 Gorges food	34 Overly preoccupied
14 Resists comfort	10 Prefers adults	26 Reaction losing friend	28 Panic attacks	7 Hides food	35 Age-inappropriate
16 Alone in the world	11 Prefer older youths	32 Reaction to criticism	29 Amnesia	18 Steals food	36 Tries to initiate sex
21 Withdrawn	13 Strangers as family	33 Life not worth living	30 Head-banging		
	19 Friendly strangers	37 Uncontrollable rage			
	20 Pleases peers				
___ Total I	___ Total II	___ Total III	___ Total IV	___ Total V	___ Total VI

TOTAL SHORT FORM SCORE (total score = sum of scale scores)

Scale I ___
Scale II ___
Scale III ___
Scale IV ___
Scale V ___
Scale VI ___

=

___ Total Short Form Score

ACA-SF scores should only be interpreted and reported by qualified child clinicians.

The Assessment Checklist for Adolescents Short Form – ACA, ACA-SF, and ACA-SF profile sheet © 2012 are copyright of the author.
Restrictions on the use of the ACA are listed in the accompanying limited licence. Unauthorised copying or distribution of paper or electronic forms is illegal.

ACA-SF Assessment Checklist for Adolescents – Short Form Profile Sheet (boys & girls) © 2012 Michael Tarren-Sweeney, PhD www.childpsych.org.uk

ID:

Young person's name:

Referral Details:

	Year	Month	Day
Date of Birth:			
Date of Assessment:			
Age:			

Carer's name:
(the person who completed the ACA)

Carer's gender: Female ☐ Male ☐

Length of time carer has known young person: _____

Carer's relationship to young person

☐ Birth parent
☐ Step-parent
☐ Grandparent
☐ Other relative
☐ Adoptive parent
☐ Foster parent
☐ Group home staff
☐ Large residential staff
☐ Youth worker
☐ Other (describe): _____

Young Person's Care Status

☐ Not in care (resides with parents)
☐ Adoption
☐ Kinship care (resides with relatives)
☐ Permanent or long-term foster care
☐ Temporary or short-term foster care
☐ Group or residential care
☐ Other (describe): _____

The Assessment Checklist for Adolescents Short Form – ACA-SF, and ACA-SF profile sheet © 2012 are copyright of the author.
Restrictions on the use of the ACA are listed in the accompanying limited licence. Unauthorised copying or distribution of paper or electronic forms is illegal.

Appendix 3

Brief Assessment Checklist for
Children (BAC-C) record form

 **Brief Assessment Checklist for Children** (ages 4 to 11)

Child's name .... Boy / Girl

Child's age ....

Your relationship to this child .... (e.g. mother, father, aunt, foster mother, grandfather)

Here are some statements that describe children's behaviour and feelings.
For each statement, please circle the number that best describes your child in the **last 4 to 6 months**.

→   circle **0** if the statement is **not true** for your child in the last 4 to 6 months.

→   circle **1** if the statement is **partly true** for your child in the last 4 to 6 months.

→   circle **2** if the statement is **mostly true** for your child in the last 4 to 6 months.

1.	0	1	2	Can't concentrate, short attention span
2.	0	1	2	Craves affection
3.	0	1	2	Eats too much
4.	0	1	2	Fears you will reject her/him
5.	0	1	2	Hides feelings
6.	0	1	2	Is convinced that friends will reject her/him
7.	0	1	2	Lacks guilt or empathy
8.	0	1	2	Prefers to be with adults, rather than children
9.	0	1	2	Relates to strangers 'as if they were family'
10.	0	1	2	Seems insecure
11.	0	1	2	Startles easily ('jumpy')
12.	0	1	2	Suspicious
13.	0	1	2	Too dramatic (false emotions)
14.	0	1	2	Too friendly with strangers
15.	0	1	2	Too jealous
16.	0	1	2	Treats you as though you were the child and she/he was the parent
17.	0	1	2	Uncaring (shows little concern for others)

For each of the following statements:

→   circle **0** if the behaviour **did not occur** in the last 4 to 6 months.

→   circle **1** if the behaviour **occurred once** in the last 4 to 6 months.

→   circle **2** if the behaviour **occurred more than once** in the last 4 to 6 months.

18.	0	1	2	Distressed or troubled by traumatic memories
19.	0	1	2	Does not show pain if physically hurt
20.	0	1	2	Sexual behaviour not appropriate for her/his age

	Office use		
U.K. English version www.childpsych.org.uk	ID:	Date:	Score:

© Michael Tarren-Sweeney, PhD, 2012. Copyright for the BAC-C is held by the author. This instrument may only be used, copied or downloaded for legitimate mental health screening, casework monitoring and research purposes. It should not be altered without the author's permission.

Appendix 4

Brief Assessment Checklist for
Adolescents (BAC-A) record form

 **Brief Assessment Checklist for Adolescents** (ages 12 to 17)

Young person's name .... Male / Female

Young person's age ....

Your relationship to this young person .... (e.g. mother, father, aunt, foster mother, grandfather)

Here are some statements that describe young people's behaviour and feelings.
For each statement, please circle the number that best describes your child in the **last 4 to 6 months**.

→ circle **0** if the statement is **not true** for this young person in the last 4 to 6 months.

→ circle **1** if the statement is **partly true** for this young person in the last 4 to 6 months.

→ circle **2** if the statement is **mostly true** for this young person in the last 4 to 6 months.

1.	**0**	**1**	**2**	Constantly seeking excitement or 'thrills'
2.	**0**	**1**	**2**	Craves affection
3.	**0**	**1**	**2**	Does not share with friends
4.	**0**	**1**	**2**	Does not show affection
5.	**0**	**1**	**2**	Feels victimised or misunderstood
6.	**0**	**1**	**2**	Gorges food
7.	**0**	**1**	**2**	Hides feelings
8.	**0**	**1**	**2**	Impulsive (acts rashly, without thinking)
9.	**0**	**1**	**2**	Lacks guilt or empathy
10.	**0**	**1**	**2**	Relates to strangers 'as if they were family'
11.	**0**	**1**	**2**	Resists being comforted when hurt
12.	**0**	**1**	**2**	Shows intense and inappropriate anger
13.	**0**	**1**	**2**	Too friendly with strangers
14.	**0**	**1**	**2**	Too jealous
15.	**0**	**1**	**2**	Tries too hard to please other young people
16.	**0**	**1**	**2**	Withdrawn

For each of the following statements:

→ circle **0** if the behaviour **did not occur** in the last 4 to 6 months.

→ circle **1** if the behaviour **occurred once** in the last 4 to 6 months.

→ circle **2** if the behaviour **occurred more than once** in the last 4 to 6 months.

17.	**0**	**1**	**2**	Appears dazed, 'spaced out' (like in a trance)
18.	**0**	**1**	**2**	Intense reaction to criticism
19.	**0**	**1**	**2**	Sexual behaviour not appropriate for her/his age
20.	**0**	**1**	**2**	Sudden or extreme mood changes

U.K. English version www.childpsych.org.uk

	Office use	
ID:	Date:	Score:

© Michael Tarren-Sweeney, PhD, 2012. Copyright for the BAC-A is held by the author. This instrument may only be used, copied or downloaded for legitimate mental health screening, casework monitoring and research purposes. It should not be altered without the author's permission.

Index